Building Wealth Through Smart Money Habits That Last

Create Long-Term Wealth Through Smarter Daily Decisions

Naomi Ellison

Table of Contents

INTRODUCTION

Building Wealth Through Smart Money Habits That Last: Create Long-Term Wealth Through Smarter Daily Decisions, rarely is financial achievement the result of good fortune or unforeseen circumstances. It is built through deliberate, disciplined, and patient daily decisions. This book examines how basic financial practices can gradually lead to long-term financial stability and greater self-assurance. It emphasizes doable steps that anyone can take, regardless of income level or current financial circumstances, rather than quick fixes or irrational claims. Each chapter aims to improve your comprehension of prudent financial decision-making while promoting behaviors that, over time, produce consistent and significant advancement.

You will learn how careful planning, deliberate spending, disciplined saving, responsible debt management, income development, investment, and financial protection all contribute to a stable future in these pages. The lessons are useful, simple to understand, and designed to help you develop habits that work for you at any stage of life. Every idea promotes long-term planning rather than short-term fixes, making financial improvement both feasible and long-lasting.

You will gain the knowledge and confidence to make better financial decisions that align with your values and aspirations as you read on. Every step you take forward enhances your ability to build long-term stability, increase your future prospects, and cultivate an attitude that sees wealth as the outcome of daily choices made with discernment, accountability, and persistence.

CHAPTER I

Money Mindset Foundations

Understanding Wealth Thinking

Many individuals think that a big pay check, a fortunate opportunity, or an inheritance are the first steps toward wealth, but long-term financial success typically starts with a person's attitude toward money. Wealth thinking is a way of thinking that influences daily decisions long before financial outcomes are apparent. Those who are already financially successful are not the only ones who can use it. Rather, it is a method of handling money with confidence, patience, purpose, and responsibility. A wealth thinker recognizes that steady habits, as opposed to abrupt breakthroughs, are the key to building financial security over time. People's attitudes toward earning, spending, saving, investing, and future planning are altered by this viewpoint. They acquire the self-control to make deliberate choices that support long-term objectives rather than responding emotionally to every financial circumstance.

Realizing that money is a tool rather than the ultimate goal is one of the most crucial aspects of wealth thinking. Money offers stability, possibilities, and choices, but it works best when spent purposefully. People who grasp this idea prioritize building a solid financial foundation over impressing others with costly things. They understand that every financial choice has long-term effects. Whether they decide to engage in personal growth, avoid needless debt, or save a portion of each pay check, they always consider whether the decisions made today will better their financial situation tomorrow.

The willingness to postpone instant gratification is a crucial component of wealth thinking. Easy finance, internet buying, and peer pressure to own the newest goods are all ways that modern culture continuously promotes rapid rewards. By urging people to prioritize long-term advantages over immediate gratification, wealth thinking opposes these drives. Delaying satisfaction does not entail living in discomfort or rejecting happiness. Rather, it entails making deliberate choices on priorities. A person may decide to invest in education rather than upgrading belongings or save money for a home rather than buying luxuries. Although these decisions frequently call for patience, they eventually produce better financial chances.

Developing personal responsibility is also necessary to comprehend wealth thinking. Because unforeseen circumstances like illness, economic downturns, or job loss can happen, financial success is not always under your control. People can, however, choose how they react to these difficulties. People with a wealth-oriented mindset look for workable answers instead of criticizing circumstances endlessly. They manage risks, cut back on wasteful spending, develop backup plans, and constantly hone their skills. They are aware that despite life's challenges, persistent work and prudent choices can progressively improve financial conditions. Instead of encouraging helplessness, this way of thinking promotes resilience.

Another crucial component of wealth thinking is learning from mistakes. Financial setbacks, whether due to bad investments, excessive spending, lost opportunities, or unforeseen circumstances, affect almost everyone at some point. Successful people view mistakes as important lessons rather than allowing them to instill fear or discouragement. They evaluate what transpired, determine more effective strategies, and put those lessons into practice going forward. This eagerness to learn keeps mistakes from happening again and boosts trust in one's finances. Every error becomes a chance to become wiser and make better decisions.

The development of wealth thinking is significantly influenced by a growth mindset. This viewpoint holds that ongoing education and practice can enhance one's financial skills and knowledge. They are aware that effective money management is a skill that takes practice rather than an innate ability. Through books, educational materials, financial conversations, and firsthand experiences, they actively seek out information. They study successful behaviors and apply them to their own life rather than thinking that affluent individuals just have unique advantages. Financial decision-making is continuously improved by this dedication to lifelong learning.

Additionally, wealth thinking pushes people to prioritize worth over beauty. Many people make the mistake of equating wealth with outward manifestations of achievement, such as fancy automobiles, high-end apparel, or costly trips. These things can be a sign of financial success for some people, but they can also be the consequence of bad financial planning or excessive borrowing. Financial stability, expanding assets, controllable debt, and the ability to make decisions in life without continual financial stress are all indicators of true prosperity. Wealth-thinking people are aware that accumulating assets is frequently more significant than flaunting one's position. Instead of overspending on transient appearances, they invest in items that will increase in value or produce money in the future.

Another characteristic that distinguishes wealth thinking is patience. It is rare for financial growth to occur overnight. Businesses take time to turn a profit, savings accounts develop slowly, investments gain value over many years, and careers frequently progress via persistent work. Individuals who are aware of this fact refrain from pursuing impractical claims of immediate financial success. They understand that tiny, repeated activities carried out consistently over extended periods of time are what lead to enduring success. They are shielded by this patience from dangerous scams that make extravagant promises without putting in the necessary work or preparation.

Wealth thinking likewise fosters confidence, but it is predicated on preparation rather than chance. Understanding one's own finances, keeping emergency funds on hand, cutting back on needless debt, and setting specific financial objectives all contribute to financial confidence. People who are prepared react coolly when unforeseen costs occur because they have made plans for uncertainty. Knowing that they have formed habits that will help them through both good and bad times boosts their confidence. This realistic assurance helps people make better decisions under pressure and lessens financial anxiety.

Keeping feelings out of financial decisions is another crucial idea. Spending and investment decisions are frequently influenced by fear, excitement, jealousy, and impatience. Someone might buy things they don't need because friends have them, or they might sell investments too soon out of fear during market turbulence. Prior to making financial decisions, wealth thinking promotes logical analysis. Before making significant decisions, people examine long-term effects, compare possibilities, ask questions, and gather information. This well-rounded strategy lowers expensive errors brought on by emotional responses.

Additionally, generosity plays a significant role in wealth thinking. Acquiring wealth is simply one aspect of financial success; another is making prudent use of resources to enhance the lives of others. Extreme wealth is not a prerequisite for generosity. A mindset of abundance rather than scarcity is reflected in even little deeds of charity, volunteer work, or support for worthy organizations. Because they understand that proper financial stewardship enables them to make more meaningful contributions to their families and communities, people who practice generosity frequently become more deliberate about managing their resources. Giving is no longer a barrier to individual achievement but rather a component of a healthy financial existence.

Setting meaningful financial objectives is another aspect of wealth thinking. Unplanned expenditure and inconsistent decision-making can quickly cause money to vanish in the absence of clear objectives. By linking daily acts to future results, goals offer motivation and direction. Whether you're saving for retirement, buying a house, paying for schooling, launching a business, or reaching financial independence, having well-defined goals promotes steady advancement. People evaluate these objectives on a regular basis, track their advancement, and modify their tactics as needed. Financial decisions are kept in line with long-term priorities and personal beliefs through this continuous process.

The sensation of control that comes from comprehending wealth thinking may be its biggest advantage. A disciplined mindset is still a solid foundation even though financial conditions, markets, and unforeseen obstacles may change. Consistently adopting prudent financial practices helps people become more resilient, confident, and capable of making better decisions over time. These characteristics frequently result in long-term financial stability that goes beyond just revenue over time. Wealth thinking turns money from a cause of stress into a tool that promotes long-term security, meaningful possibilities, and personal development. By adopting this mindset on a daily basis, people form habits that not only improve their financial situation but also enhance their general quality of life and set them up for future financial responsibility and self-assurance.

Breaking Limiting Beliefs

Many people start their financial journey with preconceived notions that subtly influence every financial decision they make. Childhood experiences, cultural customs, education, and individual achievements or shortcomings all contribute to the formation of these ideas. While some ideologies promote prudent financial practices, others erect imperceptible obstacles that impede long-term development and enduring riches. Limiting beliefs are presumptions that persuade people that riches are only accessible to a select few or that they are incapable of reaching financial success. Over time, these ideas become firmly ingrained and impact confidence, investing decisions, spending patterns, and saving practices. These ideas continue to influence financial results without the person even realizing it unless they are acknowledged and contested.

The notion that wealth is only determined by inheritance or chance is one of the most prevalent limiting ideas. People who have this belief frequently assume that they will never be financially independent by hard work alone. Because they think their efforts won't have a significant impact, they can steer clear of learning about investing, budgeting, or business opportunities. This way of thinking substitutes despondency for personal accountability. In actuality, a lot of prosperous people started out with little money and progressively accumulated riches via self-control, education, perseverance, and sound judgment. Opportunities are undoubtedly influenced by circumstances, but daily routines continue to be one of the most important determinants of long-term financial success.

Another limiting perception is that affluent people are dishonest and self-centered, or that money is intrinsically bad. Negative narratives, depictions in the media, or singular events are frequently the source of this view. Someone may unintentionally oppose financial success if they unconsciously equate riches with bad character traits because they don't want to become the kind of person they think affluent people are. Self-sabotage results from this internal struggle. Because they have fundamental ideas that becoming affluent would somehow negatively alter who they are, a person may earn more money yet spend it quickly, turn down opportunities, or avoid promotions. People can distinguish between financial resources and personal ideals when they realize that money is just a tool. Wealth can be used liberally, sensibly, and morally to enhance one's own life as well as the lives of others.

Another strong limiting notion that hinders financial success is fear of failing. Because they are afraid of making mistakes, many people are reluctant to launch a business, make stock market investments, acquire new skills, or pursue better employment. They see the worst-case scenario and let their anxiety prevent them from moving forward. However, experience-based learning is nearly always necessary for financial growth. Every professional, entrepreneur, and successful investor has faced obstacles. Failure does not determine success in the future unless individuals permit it to become irreversible. Resilience and ongoing development are promoted when errors are seen as important lessons rather than personal setbacks.

The fear of success is closely associated with the dread of failure. Though less evident, some people fear that achieving financial success will raise expectations, lead to stress, draw criticism, or cause them to become estranged from friends and family. Even when there are chances for advancement, these worries could lead them to stay in comfortable financial circumstances. Acknowledging these anxieties enables people to realize that success does not need giving up morals or interpersonal relationships. Simply put, healthy financial growth gives people more freedom to make important decisions and better serve their loved ones and communities.

The notion that financial knowledge is too complex to comprehend is another limiting perception. Some people think that personal finance, taxes, budgeting, and investing are topics that only professionals can understand. This idea inhibits education and fosters reliance on others to make crucial financial decisions. In actuality, persistent study builds financial literacy over time. Anyone can gradually increase their understanding of finance by reading books, listening to instructional materials, creating a budget, and posing intelligent questions. Every master started out as a novice who just decided to keep studying.

Another idea that restricts the generation of wealth is scarcity mentality. There is never enough money, opportunity, or achievement for everyone, according to those who have a scarcity mindset. They frequently make comparisons to others, get scared when the economy is unclear, and prioritize preventing loss over adding value. Instead of careful preparation, this viewpoint promotes defensive financial decisions motivated by worry. An abundance attitude, on the other hand, acknowledges that fresh possibilities, concepts, and abilities can consistently bring value. Abundance promotes confidence, inventiveness, and long-term thinking rather than persistent anxiety, even while it does not overlook financial concerns.

It is necessary first to become conscious of one's own ideas in order to break restricting beliefs. Due to long-standing mental patterns, many financial decisions are made automatically. Recurring financial thoughts might be used to spot trends that could no longer be beneficial to one's objectives. Declarations like "I will never be wealthy," "investing is too risky," "I am bad with money," or "people like me never succeed financially" convey beliefs rather than objective facts. Once recognized, these ideas can be challenged and swapped out for more truthful and beneficial viewpoints.

Replacing limiting ideas does not include denying reality or acting as though difficulties don't exist. Rather, it entails embracing ideas that are backed by data and personal development. For instance, substituting "I can improve my financial skills through consistent learning" for "I am bad with money" fosters a mindset that is more concerned with progress than long-term constraints. Daily activities are gradually influenced by small changes in internal language. People's confidence naturally increases and strengthens better views when they have positive experiences with budgeting, saving, investing, or earning more money.

Limiting ideas can also be changed by surrounding oneself with good financial influencers. Spending time with people who have sound financial practices offers support, useful guidance, and realistic examples of what is achievable. People are exposed to many perspectives on wealth through reading biographies, listening to educational programs, and taking part in financial conversations. It is simpler to replace outmoded ideas with viewpoints that promote accountability, opportunity, and development in positive circumstances.

Belief transformation is further strengthened by establishing realistic financial goals. When big financial goals are seen as a single destination, they may seem overwhelming. Regular possibilities for success are created when objectives are broken down into smaller milestones. Developing an emergency fund, paying off a credit card, raising monthly savings, or picking up a new investing strategy are examples of concrete evidence that success is achievable. Every success increases confidence in future successes while undermining limiting ideas from the past.

Breaking limiting beliefs is another key function of gratitude. Feelings of shortage and discouragement are frequently reinforced by a persistent focus on financial inadequacies. Gratitude exercises help people focus on the possibilities, connections, abilities, and resources they now have that can help them succeed in the future. Financial difficulties cannot be solved by gratitude, but it does provide a stronger emotional basis for sound decision-making. Instead of getting disheartened by short-term losses, people who value their existing success are frequently more motivated to keep getting better.

Since significant financial change seldom occurs overnight, developing patience is also crucial. When people are discouraged by slow progress and anticipate instant results, many limiting beliefs get stronger.

Building wealth requires long-term, persistent habits. While saving consistently, investing steadily, cutting back on wasteful spending, developing professional abilities, and making careful financial decisions may seem insignificant on their own, when combined, they produce amazing long-term outcomes. Even when apparent progress is sluggish, patience enables people to stay dedicated.

Another crucial component of overcoming limiting beliefs is personal responsibility. Taking accountability does not entail holding oneself accountable for every financial setback. Rather, it entails acknowledging the ability to affect future results independent of past events. Instead of encouraging helplessness, concentrating on acts that are under one's control promotes empowerment. Every wise financial choice, regardless of size, strengthens the basis for future prosperity.

In the end, overcoming limiting beliefs is a continuous process that involves substituting knowledge for fear, confidence for doubt, and justifications for deliberate action. Financial decisions naturally become more deliberate and consistent as healthier ideas solidify. People start to see opportunities differently, deal with obstacles resiliently rather than discouragingly, and make decisions that support long-term financial objectives. A mindset that believes growth is possible, learning never stops, and every prudent decision made today contributes to greater financial freedom tomorrow is just as important to creating lasting wealth as income or investment gains.

Building Positive Habits

Good habits are the cornerstone of long-term financial success because they impact daily choices that progressively mold a person's destiny. Even though big financial events like getting a promotion, buying a house, or investing might have a big impact on wealth, it's the little everyday actions that decide if such possibilities result in long-term success. Over time, every decision made about planning, saving, spending, and resource management affects financial results. Developing positive habits entails purposefully repeating behaviors that promote stability, accountability, and development until they become second nature. Because they gradually develop into automatic behaviors that direct prudent financial decisions, these habits lessen the need for ongoing motivation.

Understanding that significant change seldom occurs overnight is the first step towards forming positive habits. Because they anticipate quick outcomes from new financial practices, many people lose hope. They might begin saving with great enthusiasm for a few weeks, only to be let down when their account balance increases slowly. Some people might make a budget but give it up when they run into unforeseen costs. Because the advantages of positive habits take time to manifest, they demand patience. Consistently making small changes generally results in greater long-term success than short-lived, dramatic efforts. One of the best predictors of future financial success is the ability to stay dedicated in the face of sluggish growth.

When forming good habits, consistency is more important than perfection. Many people think that in order to succeed, they must adhere to every financial plan exactly. On the other hand, long-term development is not negated by sporadic errors. Making an unwise purchase or missing a month's worth of savings goals does not equate to failure. The most important thing is to get back to productive habits as soon as possible. While people who let transient errors turn into long-term habits frequently find it difficult to restore momentum, those who remain consistent in the face of sporadic setbacks continue to advance. Rather than flawless performance, positive habits are strengthened by regular practice.

Developing enduring habits requires self-awareness. It is beneficial for people to honestly assess their present financial practices before making significant changes. They could see patterns of hasty buying, irregular saving, pointless subscriptions, or sentimental purchases that subtly impede their financial advancement. The goal of identifying these behaviors is to find possibilities for improvement rather than to instill guilt. Awareness enables people to swap out harmful habits for more beneficial ones. Better decisions are easier to make after spending patterns become apparent since they are founded on knowledge rather than conjecture.

When positive behaviors are linked to significant personal objectives, they become simpler to sustain. Saving money just because it feels like the right thing to do might only serve as short-term motivation. Saving for a child's schooling, a family home, retirement security, or financial independence, on the other hand, strengthens the emotional bond. People are more willing to accept short-term compromises when their regular routines support important aims. Instead of just adhering to a regulation, every wise financial choice becomes a step toward accomplishing something personally meaningful.

Establishing routines that facilitate wise decision-making is another necessary step in developing positive habits. Structured processes are more important for successful financial management than willpower. Routines that lessen forgetfulness and impulsive behavior include setting aside time each week to evaluate costs, setting up automated savings transfers, paying bills on schedule, and monitoring financial objectives. These techniques reduce the number of tough choices that need to be made on a regular basis, which makes money management easier. People rely on routines that regularly direct productive actions rather than daily motivation.

Thoughtful spending is another beneficial habit. It is not necessary to give up enjoyment or refrain from making any purchases in order to adopt sound financial practices. Rather, they promote deliberate spending that is in line with individual interests and values. People learn to consider whether a purchase would help them achieve their long-term objectives or only fulfill a short-term want before making a purchase. This straightforward pause frequently discourages wasteful spending while fostering gratitude for things that actually enhance quality of life. People can enjoy their money without jeopardizing their future financial security by making intentional purchases.

One of the most effective strategies for creating long-term wealth is consistent saving. Over time and with consistency, even small efforts gain significance. Regular savers become more financially flexible because they plan for both anticipated and unforeseen costs. Savings provide chances for future investments and lessen reliance on borrowing in times of need. More significantly, saving is a habit that boosts confidence and discipline. Instead of focusing on immediate consumption, each donation signifies a commitment to future well-being.

Another beneficial habit that promotes financial success is lifelong learning. Technology, career needs, investment opportunities, and economic situations all change throughout time. People who are inquisitive and dedicated to learning are better able to adjust to changing conditions. Through reading, taking classes, speaking with seasoned people, and gaining real-world experience, they pursue knowledge. Understanding investing is only one aspect of financial education. It also entails learning how to solve problems effectively, boosting productivity, enhancing career capabilities, and improving communication skills. Opportunities are increased, and costly errors are decreased through ongoing learning.

Controlling one's emotions when making financial decisions is another good habit. Spending and investment practices are frequently influenced by fear, enthusiasm, frustration, and comparison. Disappointing outcomes are often the consequence of emotional buying, panic selling, or chasing false chances. Making it a habit to wait before making important financial decisions enables feelings to subside and reason to direct behavior. Before allocating financial resources, this methodical technique promotes a thorough assessment of the risks, advantages, and long-term effects.

By promoting contentment with current circumstances while still striving for future progress, gratitude supports sound financial practices. People who consistently value what they already have are frequently less under pressure to outspend others in order to compete. Gratitude lessens the impact of advertising, material expectations, and social comparison. Grateful people acknowledge their success and make financial decisions with confidence rather than insecurity, as opposed to continuously dwelling on what is lacking. More overall pleasure and better spending practices are encouraged by this balanced viewpoint.

Additionally, accountability plays a major role in the development of enduring habits. Sharing financial objectives with a dependable friend, mentor, or family member fosters accountability and support. Frequent conversations regarding advancements, difficulties, and successes offer inspiration during trying times. Accountability provides perspective and support rather than condemnation or judgment. Knowing that someone else is aware of financial objectives frequently boosts dedication and lessens the chance of giving up constructive behaviors when challenges occur.

Developing good habits affects more aspects of life than only one's financial situation. Financial success is influenced by a number of factors, including personal discipline, strong relationships, efficient time management, and good health. People who effectively manage their time tend to be more productive at work. Maintaining excellent health may lower medical costs and enhance professional effectiveness. Proficient communication abilities lead to more favorable career prospects and more robust financial collaborations. These interrelated behaviors result in a way of living that fosters both financial and personal development.

Another important quality while creating healthy behaviors is flexibility. Career changes, family responsibilities, economic adjustments, and unforeseen obstacles all unavoidably alter life situations. Good habits should adjust to these shifts without losing sight of their fundamental goals. A person who is temporarily struggling financially could cut back on their monthly savings contributions. This adaptability acknowledges real-world constraints while maintaining consistency. Long-term commitment is strengthened, and resilience is increased when routines are maintained in the face of changing circumstances.

Positive behaviors are also reinforced when progress is celebrated. Since financial accomplishment sometimes happens gradually, it's simple to miss significant advancements. Acknowledging achievements like debt repayment, savings targets, income growth, or regular budget adherence boosts motivation. Expensive prizes are not necessary for these festivities. Merely recognizing advancements boosts self-esteem and strengthens the conviction that consistent efforts eventually yield significant outcomes. Positive reinforcement makes the journey more pleasurable and motivates sustained effort.

Creating a lifestyle that inherently promotes financial well-being is the ultimate goal of developing positive habits. People establish daily routines that gradually advance them toward more stability and independence rather than depending on sporadic motivational outbursts or drastic shifts. Every wise choice, no matter how tiny, strengthens the financial future. Over the course of months and years, these consistent behaviors develop into strong forces that mold character, boost self-esteem, and open doors that would not have been possible otherwise. Through perseverance, consistency, careful decision-making, and a dedication to ongoing personal development, positive habits turn financial success from an unpredictable goal into a predictable result. People build a solid foundation for long-term prosperity, increased peace of mind, and the capacity to make better financial decisions at every stage of life by engaging in these routines on a daily basis.

The First Step Forward

All significant financial changes start long before an investment yields profits or a bank account expands. The way a person views money, opportunity, responsibility, and the future is where it all begins. The concepts discussed in this chapter serve as the cornerstone for all upcoming financial decisions. Poor decisions, emotional spending, and irregular planning may make even a high salary disappear in the absence of a good mindset. However, with the correct attitude, common choices can become potent building blocks for remarkable outcomes. This chapter is important because it moves the focus from temporary solutions to long-term personal transformation. Rarely is wealth produced by a single, spectacular occurrence. Rather, it develops as a result of thousands of little, deliberate choices made over many months and years. Every investment, financial objective, saving habit, and purchase is a reflection of an underlying view about the use of money. Financial development is far more attainable when such beliefs become optimistic, disciplined, and future-focused.

A person's bank balance is not the only thing that is altered by applying the concepts learned in this chapter. It alters self-assurance, judgment, emotional fortitude, and long-term planning. Individuals who consciously improve their financial thinking start to see chances that they had previously overlooked. They become more driven by long-term objectives and less swayed by fleeting pleasures. They learn to swap out uncertainty for planning and excuses for accountability. They start making decisions that stop financial issues before they start rather than responding to them after they arise. This proactive strategy establishes stability in all facets of life. Relationships strengthen as a result of fewer financial disputes, families experience less financial stress, and future planning becomes an exciting potential rather than a terrifying uncertainty. Because financial confidence frequently fosters greater personal confidence as well, the advantages go beyond money.

If these teachings are ignored, the results are drastically different. Financial habits frequently do not alter despite increases in income or outside chances when negative ideas are not challenged. Someone might still think that investing is solely for the wealthy, that saving is impossible, or that luck is the only factor in financial success. These ideas subtly affect day-to-day choices until years go by with little to no advancement. Small, pointless purchases start to become the norm. Because instant enjoyment is more satisfying than future security, debt increases. Because planning was never prioritized, financial emergencies become overwhelming. These recurring behaviors eventually lead to annoyance, disappointment, and needless suffering. Loss of money is not the true consequence of an unhealthy mindset. It is the loss of opportunities, autonomy, self-assurance, and tranquility that could have been attained by making deliberate decisions.

Numerous everyday circumstances demonstrate the practical effects of altering one's perspective on finance. A person who used to spend every extra dollar right away can start saving even a small sum every pay period. Another person who was afraid of investing can progressively educate themselves until they are confident in their ability to make wise choices. A person who worries about finances all the time could form budgeting habits that give them confidence instead of anxiety. Although these changes seldom occur suddenly, each wise choice builds momentum for the next. Success encourages healthy behaviors, which makes progress simpler. Things that formerly took resolve eventually become second nature. This is the long-term impact of having a sound financial mindset. It turns sporadic discipline into a regular lifestyle.

By the end of this chapter, you will be able to identify the beliefs that shape your financial decisions, swap out limiting ideas with constructive ones, develop daily routines that promote steady financial advancement rather than fleeting motivation, and develop a mindset that promotes long-term planning, disciplined decision-making, and enduring financial confidence.

Consider Daniel, a young office worker with a meager wage who thought that riches were only available to those who were fortunate enough to be born. He thought conserving so little money would never make a difference, so he rewarded himself every payday with pricey dinners, internet shopping, and impulsive purchases. Daniel questioned such a notion after discovering the potential power of thought. He began questioning whether every purchase brought him closer to or farther away from the future he desired. He instinctively set aside a tiny portion of each pay check rather than spending every extra peso.

While commuting, he read books on personal finance and honed skills that led to a promotion. His financial circumstances had dramatically improved five years later because of his savings, investments, and increased income. The amount of money he had was not the most significant shift. It was how he made all of his financial decisions. Long before his salary rose, his success started the instant he shifted his perspective.

A straightforward tale of two neighbors who planted fruit trees on the same day illustrates a similar point. When no fruit showed up in the first several months, the first neighbor quickly lost interest in watering the tree and only did so when it was convenient. He eventually lost all interest in it. The second neighbor gave the tree regular waterings, shielded it from storms, pulled weeds from its roots, and waited patiently through each season. The two trees didn't appear to be all that different at first. But years later, one tree was robust and bearing fruit, while the other had died. The development of financial habits is similar. Consistent care eventually yields effects that appear spectacular to people who only notice the end harvest, even if the results are sometimes unnoticeable at first.

Building a sturdy bridge is a helpful metaphor for financial growth. Every bridge relies on a strong base that is concealed beneath the surface. Because they are concentrating on the road above, drivers seldom ever notice the concrete supports. Nevertheless, no matter how lovely the bridge looked, it would inevitably collapse without those invisible supports. That secret foundation is your financial thinking. The obvious path is represented by savings accounts, investments, profitable ventures, and increasing wealth, but these things can only stay steady if they are underpinned by good behaviors and disciplined attitudes. Although strengthening the invisible foundation might not result in immediate praise or recognition, it does provide the steadiness required to securely navigate life's shifting circumstances and achieve all future financial success.

Use the Mindset to Momentum Framework to start putting these ideas into practice right away. Determine your present financial beliefs first. Put your regular thoughts regarding earning, spending, saving, investing, and wealth in writing. Be totally truthful without passing judgment on yourself. Next, assess each belief by determining if it fosters development or imposes constraints. Every limiting notion should be replaced with a pragmatic assertion based on possibility and accountability. Continue by deciding on one daily financial behavior that reinforces your new conviction, such as going over your spending every night, setting up an automatic savings account after each pay check, or waiting twenty-four hours before making a purchase. Continue to practice that behavior until it is no longer forced but rather automatic. At the conclusion of each week, evaluate your progress by noting advancements, recognizing obstacles, and modifying your strategy as needed. Lastly, improve current financial habits and add one new one each month to repeat the process. These repeated behaviors eventually build a system that keeps working even when motivation naturally fluctuates.

This framework's simplicity is what makes it effective. Many people fail because they try to make all the changes at once. Dramatic action is rarely necessary for long-lasting improvement. It calls for constant action. Daily repetition of little habits transforms behavior and identity over time, making them powerful. Every wise financial choice you make strengthens the idea that managing your finances responsibly is a part of who you are rather than something you only sometimes try. Because actions are linked to personal values rather than fleeting emotions, this identity-based approach promotes long-term consistency.

As you proceed, keep in mind that obstacles do not undo your progress. Everybody has unforeseen costs, shifting priorities, and depressing moments. The ability to grow from mistakes and keep going forward is what distinguishes long-term success from long-term difficulty, not the lack of mistakes. Every time you react sensibly rather than emotionally, your financial confidence increases. Every obstacle turns into a chance to hone your discipline, enhance your preparation, and gain a deeper comprehension of sound money management. Consistency, not perfection, should always be used to gauge progress.

Consider whether the financial decisions you make on a daily basis represent the future you truly wish to build. Which financial belief has hindered your success the most, and how can you replace it with a more positive outlook? In five years, what one practice might you start now that would still help your finances? If you constantly adhered to the ideas you have learned, how would your relationships, opportunities, and peace of mind improve? What promise are you ready to make now that you will be grateful for tomorrow?

Every long-lasting accomplishment starts with a deliberate choice that is followed by another. Those with ideal circumstances, exceptional talent, or limitless wealth are not the only people who can achieve financial success. It belongs to people who behave with purpose and continuously align their convictions. Every deliberate decision improves your capacity to handle difficulties, spot opportunities, and stick with your objectives in the face of transient setbacks. With perseverance, self-control, and confidence, keep building on the foundation laid here. Every step you take forward, no matter how tiny it may seem now, moves you closer to a future characterized by security, freedom, opportunity, and the long-lasting satisfaction of knowing that your everyday choices are shaping the life you genuinely choose rather than being shaped by financial instability.

CHAPTER II

Financial Goal Clarity

Defining Life Priorities

Since every financial decision reflects a person's values, defining life priorities is one of the most crucial elements in achieving long-term financial success. In the absence of defined priorities, money is frequently directed away from significant long-term objectives and toward transient desires, impulsive expenditures, or fleeting satisfaction. Many people put forth a lot of effort to make a living, yet they still find it difficult to accumulate wealth because their spending patterns are unrelated to the kind of life they really want to lead. Knowing one's own priorities gives one direction and makes it simpler to make confident decisions about how to earn, save, spend, and invest. People with clear priorities make deliberate choices that advance their intended future rather than responding to every chance or temptation.

Priorities in life go much beyond monetary objectives. Family, health, education, personal development, relationships, career fulfillment, community involvement, and personal values are among them. Instead of becoming a priority in and of itself, money should support these priorities. Financial resources are important because they offer possibilities to live in accordance with firmly held ideas, eliminate needless stress, and provide options. People are less inclined to compare themselves to others or lead lives that are intended to impress rather than satisfy when they are aware of what matters most. This change promotes financial choices that result in true contentment rather than fleeting thrills.

Financial frustration is a common result of people pursuing objectives that do not really belong to them. Expensive mansions, high-end cars, stylish clothes, and lavish vacations are frequently portrayed by society as indicators of prosperity. These comparisons are frequently magnified by social media, which puts pressure on people to keep up appearances regardless of their financial situation. Without well-defined objectives, people could spend more than they can afford in an effort to live up to expectations set by others. Debt, tension, and a delay in financial advancement are frequently the outcomes of this activity. Establishing personal priorities enables people to discern between genuine personal goals and outside pressures.

Honest self-reflection is the first step towards defining priorities. Asking oneself what kind of life they want to live for the next five, ten, or twenty years is beneficial. Some people might prefer to spend more time with their families than continuously advancing their careers. Others might place a higher priority on travel, education, entrepreneurship, philanthropy, or early retirement. Since everyone defines fulfillment differently, there is no one definition of financial success. Making sure that financial decisions constantly support personally significant goals rather than fleeting diversions is crucial.

When financial habits are linked to important priorities, they become much easier to maintain. Over time, saving money to build up a bigger bank account could feel constrictive. However, every deposit has a clear purpose when it is used to fund children's education, buy a home, become financially independent, or increase work freedom. When goals are linked to personal values, people are more motivated because they know why their daily sacrifices are important. Discipline becomes a significant investment in the future when it has a purpose.

Recognizing that not every objective merits equal attention at every stage of life is another necessary step in defining life priorities. Naturally, priorities change when conditions do. Young adults might prioritize their education, professional growth, and achieving financial security. Raising children, buying a house, and safeguarding family finances may be priorities for parents. Planning for retirement, preparing for health care, and creating a legacy may become more crucial as one ages. Regularly reviewing priorities guarantees that financial decisions stay in line with evolving possibilities and obligations rather than depending on antiquated presumptions.

Making better decisions is one of the main advantages of having well-defined priorities. Due to the limited nature of resources like money, time, and energy, every financial decision entails trade-offs. Even straightforward choices become challenging when priorities are ambiguous because each choice seems equally significant. People frequently make emotional purchases that are at odds with long-term aims, abandon budgets, or change their goals. By offering a solid framework, clear priorities make these choices easier. Before making significant financial commitments or purchases, people should consider whether the choice would advance or detract from their top priorities.

Setting priorities also makes one more resilient when faced with financial difficulties. People frequently need to modify their financial plans due to unforeseen costs, economic uncertainties, career changes, or market swings. These difficulties might lead to anxiety and perplexity if priorities are unclear. People are more equipped to make deliberate changes while safeguarding their top priorities when they know what is really important. They can temporarily put off less crucial objectives without losing sight of their main course. Financial planning can stay steady even in turbulent times because of this flexibility.

Open communication about life priorities is beneficial for relationships as well. Family members' differing views on spending, saving, and future objectives can lead to financial disputes. More understanding and collaboration are fostered by open discussions about common priorities. Budgets, savings plans, and investment strategies that represent shared objectives rather than conflicting expectations are more likely to be developed by couples who routinely discuss their financial values. Families that engage kids in age-appropriate conversations about priorities also contribute to the development of sound financial practices for coming generations.

By assisting people in differentiating between requirements, wants, and worthwhile investments, setting priorities promotes conscious spending. This awareness does not necessitate giving up pleasure or abstaining from all discretionary spending. Rather, it encourages deliberate decisions that support long-term goals and optimize enjoyment. When purchases are based on personal ideals rather than fleeting impulses, spending becomes more fulfilling. People may prioritize relationships, education, health, and meaningful experiences over material belongings.

Clearly defined life priorities also have an impact on career decisions. A higher wage is important, but it's not the only factor in financial success. Some people choose to take lower-paying jobs that offer more freedom, healthier workplaces, or better levels of personal fulfillment. Others seek further education or professional development because these chances help them achieve their larger life objectives. Establishing priorities enables people to assess career prospects based on total life satisfaction rather than just financial gain.

Since time is one of the most valuable personal resources, time management and financial priorities are strongly related. People who are aware of their priorities make more deliberate use of their time. They understand that each hour spent engaging in worthwhile pursuits adds to long-term satisfaction. Similarly, time that may be used for financial advancement or personal development is wasted on pointless distractions, excessive shopping, and continual comparing. Maintaining health, pursuing meaningful experiences, making a living, and taking care of relationships may all be balanced by scheduling time according to priorities.

Gratitude increases dedication to one's own priorities. The urge to continuously pursue worldly goods that provide only fleeting satisfaction is lessened when one appreciates existing development. While leaving space for development and progress, gratitude promotes contentment. Because they are less motivated by envy, scarcity, or outside approval, people who value what they already have frequently make better financial decisions.

Consistent financial practices over many years are supported by this emotional stability.

Another crucial trait for living in accordance with well-defined priorities is patience. Before noticeable benefits are seen, many worthwhile financial objectives need years of steady work. Building investments, buying a house, saving for retirement, or achieving financial independence seldom happen quickly. People who have defined priorities stay dedicated because they know why their everyday efforts are important in the long run. When short-term gains clash with their larger goals, they are less likely to give up on their ambitions.

Establishing a balance between financial conduct and personal beliefs is the ultimate goal of defining life objectives. Every dollar earned is a chance to fund the life that one genuinely desires. Financial decisions become less stressful when priorities are clear because they are driven by purpose rather than uncertainty. Long-term planning becomes more feasible, saving becomes more significant, investing gets more concentrated, and spending becomes more deliberate. People take charge of their financial decisions with assurance and clarity rather than letting external factors or events dictate their course. As wealth becomes a tool for sustaining the life that matters most rather than an end in itself, this alignment eventually results in both increased financial security and a deeper sense of joy.

Creating Clear Targets

Since any significant accomplishment starts with a clear direction, setting clear goals is one of the most crucial elements in creating long-term financial success. Making consistent decisions and tracking progress become challenging in the absence of a clear target. Many people put in a lot of effort and make money, but because their financial efforts are not focused, they frequently feel as though they are not making progress. By tying everyday actions to long-term goals, clear targets give every financial decision a purpose. They turn amorphous aspirations into workable strategies that may be pursued with assurance and tenacity. People who set clear goals know exactly what they are aiming for and why those goals are important, as opposed to merely hoping for more financial security.

Because they provide daily routines with a feeling of meaning, financial goals serve as a source of motivation. Consistently investing, cutting back on wasteful spending, and saving money become simpler when these activities are linked to important goals. A person is more likely to maintain discipline if they are saving for a family home, a child's education, retirement, or financial independence. Clearly defined goals serve as a reminder to people that every prudent financial decision leads to something worthwhile down the road. This sense of purpose keeps one committed even in the face of obstacles or slow progress.

Clarity is a key component of successful financial goals. Words like "wanting to become wealthy" or "improving finances" are too general to offer much useful advice. Clearly defined goals specify precisely what must be done, how much is needed, and when progress should be assessed. A person may choose to accumulate an emergency fund equal to six months' worth of living expenses within a specific time frame rather than stating that more savings are required. Because every financial decision can be evaluated in relation to a certain goal, this degree of clarity facilitates planning. Well-defined objectives minimize ambiguity and offer a useful course of action.

Setting reasonable goals is just as crucial. While unreasonable expectations frequently result in frustration and despair, ambitious goals can spur growth. Rather than abrupt, drastic improvements, financial success typically comes through incremental improvement. Establishing attainable goals enables people to make consistent progress and boost their self-esteem. Little victories build momentum that motivates more work. Larger financial goals become more achievable as confidence increases since they are backed by dependable routines and collected expertise. Setting realistic goals promotes perseverance as opposed to disappointment.

Long-term success feels more achievable when big financial goals are divided into smaller phases. When considered as a single endeavor, a major goal like buying a house or achieving financial independence may appear daunting. By breaking that goal down into smaller monthly or annual milestones, people can focus on taking immediate action instead of getting frustrated by the amount of work still to be done. Every milestone reached shows progress and strengthens the conviction that greater accomplishments are achievable with perseverance and perseverance. This methodical approach turns lofty goals into realistic everyday choices.

Putting financial goals in writing increases accountability and dedication. Objectives that are only remembered are frequently overlooked or superseded by more pressing issues. A visible reminder of one's own priorities is produced by documenting financial goals. Written goals make it simpler to assess progress over time and promote frequent reassessment. Many successful people review their objectives on a regular basis, changing tactics when conditions change while staying dedicated to the general course. Instead of making financial planning a sporadic activity, this practice maintains it ongoing.

Knowing one's own values is also necessary for setting clear goals. Instead of merely adhering to social norms or comparing accomplishments with those of others, financial goals should represent what is truly important to the individual. While some people place a higher priority on early retirement, others place a higher value on education, travel, charitable giving, owning a business, or giving family members financial security. Because they reflect meaningful desires rather than outside pressure, goals based on personal values foster more motivation. People are more inclined to uphold discipline and make deliberate decisions when their financial goals coincide with their sincerely held priorities.

Balancing short-term, medium-term, and long-term goals is another crucial component of setting financial aims. Short-term objectives give quick guidance and boost self-esteem through regular success. Larger purchases, professional promotion, or debt reduction are common medium-term objectives that call for years of work. Retirement, financial independence, asset preservation, and leaving a lasting legacy are the main long-term objectives. Sustaining equilibrium throughout these periods guarantees that current requirements are met without compromising prospects for the future. By developing a thorough financial strategy, each category helps the others.

Maintaining certain financial goals requires flexibility. Seldom does life go exactly as planned. Adjustments may be necessary along the road due to changes in one's career, financial circumstances, obligations to one's family, health issues, and unforeseen costs. Good financial planning understands that goals don't always need to be abandoned when circumstances change. Rather, people continue to pursue the same basic goal while making changes to deadlines, savings amounts, or tactics. Despite life's uncertainties, this flexibility enables financial strategies to stay current and realistic.

Financial goals are kept relevant and attainable with the support of regular progress reviews. Without regular assessment, people might keep using inefficient tactics or miss chances to get better. Examining financial objectives on a monthly or quarterly basis gives important information about what is doing well and what needs to be adjusted. These evaluations promote candid introspection, recognize successes, point out challenges, and reaffirm dedication to ongoing advancement. Financial planning is no longer a one-time event but rather a continuous process thanks to consistent evaluation.

Setting specific goals also aids in lowering rash financial decisions. Unnecessary purchases are easier to avoid when people know exactly what they are aiming for because every purchase is weighed against future priorities. The focus now switches from whether an item is appealing to whether it advances or postpones significant financial goals. This straightforward shift in viewpoint promotes intentional spending and strengthens discipline. People make decisions that are consistent with their predetermined goals rather than impulsively responding to commercials or social pressure.

As people reach their financial goals, their confidence naturally increases. Each goal accomplished shows that disciplined habits yield significant outcomes. A person's confidence in their ability to handle money is strengthened when they pay off debt, attain a savings goal, increase their investment contributions, or successfully stick to a budget. Because they have seen the benefits of persistent work, people are motivated to seek more ambitious goals as their confidence grows. Because it is backed by actual experience, confidence derived from accomplishment is more resilient than confidence derived solely from optimism.

Setting financial goals promotes personal development in addition to money management. Pursuing meaningful goals frequently necessitates learning new financial concepts, enhancing professional abilities, boosting productivity, improving communication, and fortifying self-discipline. People often grow more resilient, patient, and organized as they strive toward their financial objectives. These character traits lead to more chances for professional growth, improved relationships, and increased success all around. As a result, financial planning serves as a stimulus for more extensive personal growth.

Improved decision-making in ambiguous circumstances is another important advantage of setting explicit goals. Without a defined plan, market swings, economic shifts, and unforeseen financial possibilities can cause confusion. People who have goals assess new circumstances based on how well they align with their long-term ambitions. Before making significant decisions, this clarity promotes careful consideration and lessens emotional reactions. Instead of pursuing every chance or responding to every obstacle, they stay concentrated on tactics that continuously help them achieve their goals.

When financial goals are clear and significant, perseverance becomes simpler. Every long-term objective has times of sluggish development, unforeseen obstacles, and depressing moments. Having specific goals helps people remember why they started the journey and gives them the will to keep going even in the face of short-term setbacks. They see setbacks as brief obstacles within a much bigger process rather than as failures. This viewpoint promotes perseverance, fortitude, and a sustained dedication to sound financial practices.

In the end, setting specific goals turns financial success from an ill-defined dream into a realistic and attainable path. Establishing clear goals gives daily decisions focus, boosts motivation, promotes discipline, and makes progress quantifiable over time. They lessen distractions that impede long-term achievement while assisting people in concentrating on what really counts. Financial goals become effective guides that mold responsible behaviors and prudent choices through careful planning, reasonable expectations, frequent assessment, and consistent execution. As each objective is accomplished, people gain more self-assurance, improve their financial literacy, and gain a better comprehension of how deliberate planning produces long-term stability. Anyone may create a stronger financial future based on purpose, tenacity, and ongoing development by setting meaningful goals and sticking to them in the face of shifting conditions.

Measuring Progress

Achieving long-term financial success requires measuring progress because it turns aspirations into quantifiable achievements. When making a budget, saving money, paying off debt, or investing for the future, many people start off enthusiastically, but if they never assess their progress, their desire may wane. Progress shows that everyday routines are yielding significant outcomes. Consistent assessment shows that wise financial decisions add up over time, even when improvements seem modest. People who track their progress on a regular basis are better able to make educated decisions and have a better awareness of their financial condition rather than depending on feelings or presumptions.

Raising awareness is one of the biggest advantages of tracking progress. Financial difficulties frequently arise gradually, making it challenging to identify them without close monitoring. Spending might gradually rise, savings contributions might become erratic, or pointless subscriptions might go unreported. Frequent financial assessments assist in spotting these trends before they develop into serious issues. Positive behaviors like increasing savings, lowering debt levels, enhancing investment contributions, or developing better budgeting practices are also highlighted by regular tracking. Awareness makes it possible to recognize accomplishments and fix errors before they become expensive.

Financial advancement should always be evaluated in relation to one's own objectives rather than those of others. Each person starts from a different place, has different responsibilities, and has a different definition of success. Comparing one's financial success to that of friends, coworkers, or celebrities on social media frequently leads to unwarranted discouragement or inflated expectations. Someone else might inherit fortune, make more money, or have fewer financial responsibilities. The degree to which a person improves in comparison to their initial state is what determines meaningful growth. Even if others seem affluent, a family that regularly saves a small amount each month may be making impressive progress. Comparing oneself to others is still far less beneficial than improving oneself.

It is simpler to assess progress when there are clear financial objectives. Since success cannot be precisely evaluated, vague intentions like wanting more money or trying to become financially secure offer no advice. Establishing clear goals produces quantifiable benchmarks that motivate sustained effort. Building an emergency fund, paying off a specific debt, boosting retirement contributions, cutting back on wasteful spending, or reaching a specific investment balance are a few examples of goals. These quantifiable goals give guidance and make it simpler to identify successes along the way.

When gauging financial development, consistency is more important than perfection. After a few losses, many people lose hope because they think that one unforeseen expense or bad financial choice has wiped out all of their prior achievements. In actuality, financial progress seldom takes a straight line. Throughout life, there are emergencies, shifts in income, and unforeseen obligations. A more realistic picture of overall improvement might be obtained by tracking progress across months and years rather than concentrating solely on particular setbacks. In general, long-term consistency yields better benefits than brief bursts of flawless financial behavior followed by a break from good habits.

One of the most useful ways to gauge financial progress is still to keep track of spending. Each purchase is a choice regarding one's own priorities and the distribution of resources. Examining monthly spending trends shows if funds are continuously going toward long-term objectives or veering toward wasteful spending. People frequently find spending patterns they were unaware of, which enables them to make deliberate changes. Reduced wasteful spending eventually opens up more chances to invest, save, and become financially independent.

Another useful indicator of financial improvement is tracking the increase in savings. Seeing savings steadily rise shows that persistent discipline yields noticeable outcomes. Regular payments and long-term dedication make even small contributions meaningful. Because higher reserves lessen reliance on debt in unforeseen circumstances, savings progress also represents increased financial resilience. When people see their savings increase, they frequently feel more confident about their capacity to handle future financial difficulties.

Another useful measure of financial achievement is debt reduction. Increased financial freedom and better prospects for the future are represented by each payment made toward debt reduction. Keeping an eye on diminishing balances promotes perseverance, especially when payback takes several years. People gain from realizing how much has already been paid off rather than concentrating just on the outstanding debt. Celebrating small victories keeps motivation high and reinforces sound financial practices.

Progress on investments should also be carefully assessed. Because market prices fluctuate naturally over time, short-term performance is not a good indicator of long-term success. Disciplined investors concentrate on steady contributions, diverse portfolios, and long-term gain rather than impulsively responding to transient swings. Evaluating whether investment practices stay in line with individual objectives rather than being too preoccupied with day-to-day market fluctuations is a key component of tracking success. Compound growth can yield significant outcomes over many years with patience.

Although raising income by itself does not ensure long-term prosperity, income growth offers another helpful viewpoint on financial progress. People gain from tracking not just their income but also how well they handle increased income. Increases in income present worthwhile chances to grow savings, make more reliable investments, lower debt, or enhance financial security. However, more money could result in more spending if it is not managed carefully. Compared to pay alone, measuring how additional income helps to long-term goals offers a more relevant evaluation of financial achievement.

When assessing financial growth, personal development should also be taken into account. In addition to numbers, more understanding, better decision-making, more self-discipline, and more positive attitudes toward money are all necessary for financial success. Even before immediate financial benefits become apparent, learning about budgeting, investing, taxes, negotiating, or éntrepreneurship signifies significant advancement. The capacity to make better financial judgments throughout life is strengthened with each new skill. Assessing personal development promotes lifelong learning and acknowledges the financial value of information.

Since financial well-being encompasses both economic stability and peace of mind, emotional development merits equal consideration. Many people feel nervous, overburdened, or unsure about money when they first start their financial journey. Fear frequently gives way to confidence when good habits emerge. People become more at ease with facing unforeseen costs, making financial decisions, and establishing future plans. In addition to promoting better relationships and more emotional resilience, less financial stress enhances overall quality of life. Financial success goes beyond account balances, and measuring emotional improvement recognizes this.

Frequent financial evaluations provide chances for modification rather than condemnation. The goal of progress measurement is to enhance future selections rather than to critique previous ones. Sincere assessments assist in identifying strengths that should be maintained and deficiencies that need to be addressed. While maintaining focus on long-term goals, financial strategies should be adaptable enough to change with the times. Consistent evaluations are a crucial component of effective financial management since early adjustments frequently avert more serious issues down the road.

A key component of sustaining long-term motivation is acknowledging accomplishments. Financial objectives frequently call for years of steady work, which makes it simple to miss significant accomplishments along the way. Acknowledging accomplished milestones serves to remind people that their efforts are yielding benefits and to promote beneficial habits. Celebrations don't have to include costly prizes that impede financial advancement. While maintaining financial discipline, simple appreciation of achievements, sharing success with loved ones, or thinking back on personal development offers significant encouragement.

Since meaningful wealth builds gradually, patience is still crucial throughout the measurement process. When people contrast their current situation with lofty long-term objectives rather than acknowledging consistent progress, they may get disheartened. Measuring progress promotes appreciation for small victories while reiterating the idea that financial freedom is not achieved by abrupt, drastic changes but rather by making numerous wise choices. Over decades, minor adjustments made repeatedly frequently result in remarkable results.

In the end, tracking progress fosters confidence, accountability, and clarity. It turns financial management from a sequence of discrete choices into a deliberate process driven by facts rather than feelings. People who assess their financial practices on a regular basis become more conscious of where they are, where they want to go, and what changes are required along the route. Stronger financial security, greater resilience, and more freedom to pursue important life goals are all benefits of every positive move, no matter how small. Measuring progress becomes a powerful habit that promotes prudent daily decisions and long-term financial success by emphasizing ongoing development rather than perfection.

Turning Vision Into Action

One of the biggest advantages somebody can get is having a clear financial path because every significant achievement starts with knowing where to go. Even though many people put in a lot of effort every day, make a living, and make several financial decisions, they frequently feel as though nothing is happening. Lack of effort isn't usually the cause. It is more frequently a lack of direction. Without a goal, hard work might lead to fatigue rather than advancement. However, every financial decision gains worth when it is linked to significant objectives since it adds to something more than the here and now. This chapter is important because it turns impractical aspirations into measurable, reviewable, and attainable goals. You start building a better financial future by taking intentional action rather than just hoping for one. Having a defined destination gives you confidence when making critical decisions and inspires you throughout trying times. Instead of being consumed by transient diversions, it enables every dollar, every habit, and every opportunity to serve a higher cause.

Everyday financial decision-making is altered by putting the concepts discussed in this chapter into practice. Instead of responding emotionally to situations, you start assessing decisions based on how well they align with your long-term goals. Because needless purchases are easier to spot, spending becomes more deliberate. Because each donation shows tangible progress toward a significant goal, saving takes on greater significance. When you comprehend how further education, enhanced abilities, or new possibilities complement your intended future, career options become more evident. Because investments are chosen based on predetermined priorities rather than fleeting excitement, they become simpler to assess. When losses are perceived as transient challenges rather than irreversible failures, they can become less depressing. Progress is rarely a straight line, as someone with a clear direction knows. The destination doesn't alter, albeit adjustments can be required.

Even when income rises, disregarding these rules frequently results in frustration. Financial decisions are influenced by outside factors, convenience, or impulse when there are unclear goals. People may borrow money without thinking about the long-term effects, spend based on trends rather than priorities, or put off saving because there isn't a strong enough reason to start now. Due to the lack of a clear target, years may go by with a great deal of work but very little quantifiable progress. Opportunities could be lost because their worth was never acknowledged. When there is no more comprehensive plan to handle life's obstacles, every unforeseen expense feels overwhelming, which frequently leads to a rise in financial stress. Lack of direction makes it possible for short-term pleasures to take the place of long-term success, leaving many people perplexed as to why years of effort yielded fewer returns than anticipated.

Applying these concepts has a real-world impact that goes far beyond monetary gain. Confidence, self-control, relationships, and emotional health are all impacted by well-defined objectives. When everyone knows why financial decisions are made, families become more cohesive. Youngsters see regular behaviors that teach them responsibility on a daily basis. Because similar priorities rather than opposing emotions drive spending and saving decisions, couples have fewer arguments. Because preparation takes the place of uncertainty, people feel more at ease. Every time a milestone is accomplished, confidence increases since advancement is now apparent rather than hypothetical. Even modest successes generate momentum, which strengthens the conviction that more ambitious objectives can be attained with persistent work.

By the end of this chapter, you will be able to identify significant financial objectives that are consistent with your long-term priorities and personal values, develop practical action plans that turn lofty goals into attainable daily routines, and assess financial opportunities and choices based on whether they promote your desired future rather than fleeting feelings or external pressure.

Take Maria as an example. She always wanted a house but never thought it would be feasible. She loved occasional shopping excursions, paid her bills each month, and prayed that one day things would get better. Her dream never materialized into a clear goal; thus, it remained far away. She made the decision one afternoon to figure out how much she needed to save each month, how long she wanted to attain that goal, and how much she needed for a down payment. She turned yearly bonuses into savings, cut back on pointless subscriptions, and took on freelance work on the weekends. Every financial choice she made became simpler since she could quickly ascertain if it advanced or postponed her goal. She had the keys to her first house four years later. In retrospect, Maria saw that choosing to replace an ill-defined ideal with a concrete plan backed by daily action—rather than signing the purchase agreement—was the most crucial moment.

The same idea is demonstrated with a short narrative. A pair of trekkers got ready to traverse a vast wilderness. The first went in without a map because he thought he would ultimately figure out the correct route by making mistakes. Before starting the voyage, the second person planned rest stops, prepared supplies, identified significant landmarks, and analyzed the route. Both hikers made progress for the first several hours, but as the routes split, the first hiker became lost and lost time going back. The second was always aware of the destination's direction and was able to adapt to unforeseen challenges. Although both put forth effort, only one continually made progress toward the intended result. The similar pattern applies to financial adventures. Progress is not assured by effort alone. Effort is transformed into significant progress when there is clear direction.

The lighthouse along a rocky coastline serves as a helpful symbol for deliberate financial preparation. Ships face shifting tides, strong storms, and unforeseen challenges, but the lighthouse stays still and offers a dependable point of reference in any weather. In daily life, financial objectives have the same function. Even while income may fluctuate, the economy may change, and unforeseen costs may occur, well-defined goals continue to offer direction. They keep uncertainty from dictating the course of your journey, but they do not eliminate every obstacle. When faced with tough choices, your objectives serve as a guiding light to assist you in selecting the safest and most effective path.

Use the Vision to Achievement Framework to start putting these concepts into practice right away. Start by deciding on one financial goal that is truly important to you, as opposed to one that is impacted by social pressure or comparison. To ensure that you understand precisely what success looks like, write it in a clear and quantifiable manner. Next, ascertain the significance of accomplishing this goal by relating it to your desired lifestyle, future security, family, or personal values. Next, create a reasonable schedule and break the overarching goal down into manageable milestones. Next, determine the daily or weekly routines needed to sustain consistent advancement, such as monitoring spending, boosting savings, cutting back on pointless purchases, or creating new revenue streams. Plan frequent monthly evaluations to track your progress, recognize your accomplishments, and modify your strategy as needed. Lastly, maintain flexibility without giving up on your goal. Although life rarely goes as planned, progress can still be made in spite of brief setbacks by regularly reviewing and making careful modifications.

This framework's strength is its capacity to turn ambitious goals into doable tasks. Many people lose hope because they only consider the size of the destination rather than the little daily choices that lead to amazing outcomes. Every accomplishment boosts self-esteem and shows that sustained work is worthwhile. Little accomplishments don't mean nothing. They are evidence that significant change is occurring. Over time, increased commitment is encouraged by momentum, which is created by consistency.

Realizing that your goals should vary as your life does is another crucial lesson. Your priorities may need to change as a result of new experiences, obligations, and possibilities. Abandoning a vision does not equate to changing a plan. While keeping an eye on the overall goal of each choice, financial planning should be adaptable. Because your long-term direction continues to drive your decisions even when short-term conditions abruptly change, this balanced approach enables you to maintain confidence in the face of uncertainty.

When accomplishments are acknowledged along the way, progress also becomes more sustainable. Celebrating accomplishments keeps you motivated and serves as a reminder that steady progress rather than big breakthroughs is the key to long-term success. Every achievement, whether it's debt repayment, savings growth, professional training, or hitting an investing milestone, merits acknowledgment since it's a step toward greater financial independence and self-assurance.

Consider whether the financial choices you are making now represent the kind of future you really want to build. Which particular financial goal should you focus on right now? Which everyday routine is keeping you from steadily moving closer to your ideal future? How would your life be better if all of your savings and spending choices were in line with your top priorities? What doable steps can you take this week to advance your long-term financial goals significantly?

Every great destination starts with a well-defined choice and steady activity. Only when dreams are backed by dedication, self-control, and deliberate decisions made repeatedly over time can they be realized. The consistent application of intentional habits that align with your highest values will decide your future financial success rather than sporadic moments of inspiration. Proceed with assurance, knowing that each deliberate choice fortifies your path and each significant action advances the realization of your ideal future. Until your goal becomes your reality, be committed, remain flexible, and keep in mind that long-term financial development is made one deliberate step at a time.

CHAPTER III

Daily Spending Awareness

Tracking Daily Expenses

One of the easiest yet most useful financial habits a person can form is keeping track of their everyday spending. Even though it might seem like a simple activity, regularly keeping track of where money is spent paints a clear picture of financial behavior and offers insightful information that cannot be obtained by memory alone. Because individual expenses can appear trivial, many people underestimate how much they spend on daily purchases. However, over the course of weeks, months, and years, tiny amounts spent consistently can add up to large sums. People can better understand their financial habits and make well-considered decisions that promote long-term financial security by keeping track of their daily expenses.

Increased awareness is one of the biggest advantages of keeping track of spending. Financial issues frequently arise gradually as opposed to abruptly. Unconsidered small expenditures might gradually deplete funds, increase dependency on borrowing, or postpone crucial financial objectives. It is simple to assume that money is vanishing for unidentified causes when there is no clear record of expenditures. This uncertainty is eliminated with expense tracking, which makes it clear where every dollar is spent. Without making significant lifestyle adjustments, this awareness enables people to spot spending patterns that may have gone unnoticed and spot chances to enhance financial management.

Keeping track of everyday spending also aids people in differentiating between needs and wants. Everybody has everyday living expenses like housing, food, transportation, medical care, and utilities. Discretionary expenditures that offer comfort, convenience, or amusement go hand in hand with these requirements. Enjoying life is perfectly acceptable, but knowing the difference between necessary and optional expenditures enables people to allocate their financial resources better. Keeping track of spending promotes careful consideration before making purchases and helps guarantee that financial choices are based on long-term goals rather than fleeting desires.

Accountability is another significant benefit of tracking expenses. People tend to be more frugal with their money when they are aware that every purchase will be documented. Because each expense is visible rather than quickly forgotten, this small act promotes greater responsibility. By establishing a clear link between financial objectives and spending choices, accountability promotes self-discipline. As people grow more conscious of how minor spending impacts overall financial development, this practice eventually organically eliminates needless purchases.

Realistic budget creation is also aided by expense tracking. Because it does not fairly represent real spending patterns, an assumption-based budget may not be successful. People can create budgets based on actual financial behavior rather than guesses by gathering comprehensive data about everyday costs. Better planning is made possible by this accuracy, which also lessens the frustration brought on by irrational expectations. A well-informed budget turns into a useful manual that takes into account the situation as it is and promotes steady improvement rather than instant perfection.

It doesn't take complex systems or in-depth financial knowledge to form the habit of keeping track of costs. While some people use spreadsheets, budgeting software, or digital banking tools, others prefer to use notebooks. Maintaining consistency is more crucial than the particular approach. The objective is to produce a trustworthy record that fairly depicts everyday expenditures. Because complex systems are more likely to be abandoned, simplicity frequently promotes long-term success. The likelihood that the habit will persist over time is increased by selecting a method that is easily incorporated into everyday routines.

Emotional spending tendencies that could otherwise go unnoticed are also revealed by tracking spending. Emotions rather than real needs drive a lot of purchases. Financial decisions can be influenced by a variety of factors, including stress, boredom, enthusiasm, loneliness, and social pressure. People may discover that particular emotions frequently result in needless purchases by routinely analyzing their spending history. Identifying these trends offers chances to produce more cost-effective, healthier solutions. This increased self-awareness promotes more deliberate financial conduct and improves emotional regulation.

Finding recurring costs is another important advantage. Regular service costs, membership fees, automatic renewals, and monthly subscriptions frequently go unnoticed for extended periods of time. Even if each payment might not seem like much, taken as a whole, they can account for a sizable amount of monthly costs. People might assess if these ongoing expenses still offer enough value by keeping track of their daily spending. Without requiring significant lifestyle compromises, cutting back on pointless subscriptions or negotiating reduced service fees might free up more funds for investments, savings, or debt reduction.

Making better financial decisions during unpredictable economic times is another benefit of tracking expenses. People must swiftly modify their spending priorities in response to rising costs, shifting incomes, or unforeseen situations. People who are already aware of their financial habits are better able to react since they are aware of which costs are necessary and which can be temporarily cut. This flexibility eases the stress of making quick financial adjustments and boosts confidence during difficult circumstances.

Keeping track of daily spending as a family has many advantages. Open communication about priorities, objectives, and spending choices is encouraged by financial transparency. Family members are more likely to recognize the value of prudent money management when they are all aware of household expenses. Expense monitoring is an educational tool that parents may use to teach kids about conserving money, creating a budget, and making careful purchases. These discussions foster sound financial practices that may be passed down through the generations and strengthen long-term financial stability.

The contribution of spending tracking to reaching financial objectives is another significant feature. Clear financial goals necessitate steady progress, whether you're saving for school, buying a house, creating an emergency fund, or getting ready for retirement. Monitoring spending makes it easier to spot places where funds can be reallocated to achieve these objectives. Over time, even little cuts to wasteful spending can add up to significant savings. People frequently find that achieving significant financial goals depends more on efficiently managing current resources than on raising income.

By substituting information for uncertainty, keeping track of spending also boosts confidence. Uncertainty over whether spending is under control frequently leads to financial stress. People who don't properly understand their financial situation may worry about money. Keeping precise expenditure records saves needless tension by providing clarity. A stronger sense of control is produced by knowing precisely how much is being spent, where changes may be made, and how progress stacks up against financial objectives. Instead of encouraging reactive behavior, this confidence promotes proactive decision-making.

Just as crucial as keeping track of expenses is the practice of routinely examining them. Although daily entries offer useful data, periodic analysis yields significant insights. People can compare expenditure categories, spot trends, and assess whether financial actions support long-term goals by conducting weekly or monthly assessments. These evaluations offer chances to recognize advancements and pinpoint areas in need of development. Frequent reflection turns tracking expenses from a record-keeping activity into an effective instrument for ongoing financial development.

When developing the habit of keeping track of costs, patience is crucial. At first, keeping track of every transaction could seem pointless or inconvenient. Like many good habits, though, it gets simpler with regular practice. People eventually start to recognize the important information their records offer. They strengthen their financial discipline, become more conscious of their spending habits, and gain confidence in their ability to handle money. The short daily time needed to keep correct records is greatly outweighed by these long-term advantages.

By promoting careful consideration before making purchases, expense tracking also helps people make appropriate decisions. People frequently start questioning whether a purchase is really essential, whether it fits with their financial priorities, and whether there is a less costly option. This quick break before spending promotes more intentionality and lessens rash judgments. Every purchase becomes a part of a bigger strategy rather than an isolated choice, which leads to the natural development of financial discipline.

In the end, keeping track of daily costs involves much more than just keeping track of figures. It is a useful habit that promotes long-term financial success, raises awareness, fortifies discipline, and enhances planning. Every expense that is documented offers important information that helps people make better decisions and feel more confident about their finances. People who regularly keep an eye on their spending acquire the knowledge necessary to manage their money instead of letting it rule them. This practice builds a solid basis for responsible money management over time, enabling people to recognize opportunities, overcome obstacles, and steadily move closer to significant financial objectives. Tracking daily costs becomes a crucial habit that promotes long-term financial stability, increased peace of mind, and a future based on deliberate daily choices rather than chance or uncertainty through perseverance, consistency, and honest self-evaluation.

Recognizing Spending Patterns

One of the most important abilities for anyone looking for long-term financial stability and enduring prosperity is the capacity to identify spending trends. Every financial choice, no matter how big or tiny, adds to a general trend that affects prospects in the future. Many people think that sporadic expensive purchases are the main cause of financial goal delays, but in actuality, daily routines that are performed frequently have a bigger effect over time. When small, seemingly inconsequential purchases are made on a regular basis, they can eventually eat up a significant amount of monthly income. People become more conscious of where their money is going and whether their financial decisions help or hinder their long-term goals by learning to recognize their own spending patterns.

Routines, habits, emotions, personal values, and contextual factors all contribute to the steady development of spending patterns. Due to their constant repetition and lack of conscious effort, many financial actions become automatic. Without careful consideration, routine behaviors like buying coffee in the morning, shopping online frequently, eating out, subscribing to entertainment services, impulsive purchases, and convenience spending could all develop. People may underestimate the whole financial cost of these habits since they frequently feel typical. Acknowledging these habitual behaviors enables people to assess whether they genuinely enhance happiness or merely waste resources that may be used for more important objectives.

Gaining a thorough understanding of income and expenses is one of the first steps in identifying spending trends. Many people are aware of their monthly income, but they only have a hazy idea of how it is allocated. Financial judgments are based on conjecture rather than facts in the absence of precise information. Consistently keeping track of spending gives important information about where money is really being spent. Surprising trends, such as categories where expenditure consistently surpasses expectations, are frequently revealed by this technique. Rather than responding to financial stress after it happens, awareness provides the chance to make well-informed adjustments.

Spending behavior is significantly influenced by emotions. Many purchases are driven by emotions like tension, boredom, excitement, grief, loneliness, or celebration rather than necessity. The underlying emotional need is rarely met by emotional spending, which frequently offers momentary solace or fulfillment. People may feel regret after the emotional moment has passed, but they still have to deal with the financial fallout from their choices. It is easier to distinguish between true needs and emotional impulses when one is able to identify emotional triggers. Because of this understanding, people can learn healthier coping mechanisms for their emotions without turning to wasteful purchasing.

Modern marketing and advertising also have a subtle but significant impact on consumer spending habits. Companies spend a lot of money on eye-catching displays, time-limited promotions, tailored suggestions, and emotive messages to entice customers to buy. Advertising is now more targeted than ever thanks to digital technology, which exposes people to goods and services according to their interests and past purchasing habits. Without realizing it, people might start buying things because they are constantly exposed to them rather than because they actually need them. The capacity to make independent financial decisions based on personal priorities rather than outside influence is strengthened by being aware of these factors.

Spending patterns are further shaped by social influences. Expectations about lifestyle choices, fashion, entertainment, cuisine, travel, and technology are frequently set by friends, coworkers, family, and online communities. Instead of making purchases that are in line with their financial objectives, many people spend money to keep up appearances or to prevent feeling left behind. Comparing one's lifestyle to that of others puts undue strain on oneself and promotes overspending. Understanding the impact of social comparison enables people to concentrate on their own financial journey rather than continuously gauging achievement in relation to outside norms.

Another prevalent trend that needs close examination is impulse buying. Impulsive purchases are frequently made without much deliberation and are motivated more by instant gratification than by careful contemplation. Frequent impulsive buying steadily diminishes the resources available for saving, investing, and accomplishing long-term goals, even while sporadic spontaneous purchases might not result in serious financial issues. Making it a habit to stop before making unnecessary purchases frees up important time for introspection. This straightforward delay frequently promotes more deliberate financial decisions and lessens emotional decision-making.

Long-term financial advancement is likewise impacted by convenience expenditure. Speed and ease are frequently prioritized in modern lifestyles, which causes consumers to pay more for services that save time or require less work. Convenience is indeed useful in many circumstances, but frequent convenience purchases can subtly raise monthly costs. Spending habits that should be regularly reviewed include ordering prepared meals rather than preparing them, paying needless delivery costs, and replacing rather than fixing serviceable objects. Acknowledging these behaviors does not need completely giving up convenience; rather, it promotes careful evaluation of whether the extra expense regularly offers adequate return.

Another area where spending trends are sometimes overlooked is subscription services. Digital storage, fitness regimens, software subscriptions, entertainment platforms, and other internet services sometimes include monthly automatic fees. Individual subscription fees are typically low, so after enrollment, they might not get much attention. On the other hand, several subscriptions spread over a number of years can add up to a significant cash outlay. Reviewing recurring costs on a regular basis guarantees that payments will continue to yield significant advantages rather than just being made out of habit.

Spending patterns that are seasonal or sporadic should also be closely monitored. Predictable financial demands are frequently created throughout the year by holidays, birthdays, vacations, school fees, and house maintenance. Instead of relying on debt or financial stress when bills come, those who are aware of these recurrent events can progressively prepare by saving in advance. When predictable costs are planned for, they become controllable components of a well-structured financial strategy rather than unforeseen difficulties.

Understanding the distinction between needs and wants is another aspect of identifying spending habits. Housing, food, healthcare, utilities, and transportation are examples of necessities that sustain daily existence and should be given the proper financial attention. Purchases that enhance ease, comfort, or enjoyment but are not essential for basic well-being are considered wants. Although all categories are valuable, people can allocate their financial resources more purposefully if they are aware of their distinctions. This distinction promotes thoughtful decision-making without removing enjoyable chances.

Spending habits are heavily influenced by personal values. Every purchase is, in part, a reflection of what a person values. Individuals who place a high value on knowledge may voluntarily spend money on books, classes, or career advancement. Health-conscious people might spend more on wholesome food, exercise, or preventative medical care. Others might value travel, spending time with family, giving to charities, or engaging in creative activities more. Determining whether one's spending patterns truly reflect one's values increases contentment while cutting back on pointless expenses that don't contribute to long-term fulfillment.

Spending habits that consistently support financial goals make them easier to attain. Regularly assessing whether current spending aligns with priorities is beneficial for anyone saving for a home, retirement, business opportunity, or emergency fund. Because funds allocated to one goal cannot concurrently support another, every financial action has an opportunity cost. Understanding this link promotes careful trade-offs that support long-term financial advancement without demanding unattainable perfection.

Regularly reviewing spending trends offers chances for ongoing development. As income, family obligations, professional prospects, and personal priorities change over time, financial habits also alter. Reviews conducted on a monthly or quarterly basis assist in identifying both areas that need improvement and favorable developments. Instead of seeing these assessments as criticism, people can see them as worthwhile educational opportunities that enhance their financial literacy and help them make better decisions in the future.

Instead of making drastic short-term adjustments, creating healthier spending habits takes time and commitment. Trying to cut every pointless expense right away frequently results in irritation and unsustainable habits. Because they enable new habits to develop into enduring patterns, gradual improvements are usually more successful. Over time, minor changes like cutting back on impulsive purchases, cooking more frequently at home, cutting back on pointless subscriptions, or boosting planned savings add up to big financial gains.

In the end, identifying spending trends enables people to take more charge of their financial future. Unconscious habits are transformed into deliberate choices driven by meaningful objectives and personal values through awareness. People take an active role in directing their financial lives rather than letting emotions, advertising, societal pressure, or convenience dictate their financial conduct. Every well-considered expenditure choice builds the groundwork for longer-term prosperity, more flexibility, and more financial stability. Financial decisions naturally become more purposeful as regular awareness becomes a daily habit, supporting not only healthier finances but also a more balanced, satisfying, and full life.

Making Better Choices

Since every financial outcome is influenced by a sequence of decisions made over time, making better judgments is one of the most crucial elements for attaining long-term financial stability. Rarely does wealth come from a single spectacular occurrence. Rather, it is frequently constructed through innumerable tiny decisions that progressively generate favorable momentum. Future opportunities are influenced by every purchase, savings contribution, investment choice, and financial commitment. Everyone has the capacity to make better decisions, even though no one can foresee every difficulty or have control over every situation. Perfection is not necessary to make better decisions. They necessitate awareness, careful thought, and a readiness to prioritize long-term achievement over short-term gratification.

Every financial decision starts with a decision between short-term gains and long-term advantages. There are several opportunities in daily life to spend money on items that provide momentary pleasure. A healthy and pleasurable existence can be enhanced by occasional rewards, but continually focusing on instant gratification frequently postpones significant financial advancement. It may take patience to decide to invest for the future, cut back on wasteful spending, or save instead of spend, but these choices eventually improve financial security. Better decisions are frequently less thrilling at first, but they eventually lead to more independence and self-assurance.

Knowing one's own priorities is one of the cornerstones of making better decisions. When people are clear about what matters most to them, making financial decisions becomes easier. While some people place a higher priority on education, travel, business prospects, retirement security, or helping family members, others place a higher value on owning a home. Money can be easily squandered on things or activities that only bring fleeting satisfaction if priorities are unclear. Financial decisions naturally become more deliberate when priorities are clear since each choice is assessed based on whether it advances significant long-term objectives.

Accurate information must be gathered before making financial commitments in order to make better decisions. People act too hastily without completely understanding the implications, which leads to many expensive blunders. Whether you're thinking about making a big purchase, taking out a loan, switching careers, or investing, thorough research offers insightful information that helps you make better choices. Costly mistakes are frequently avoided by taking the time to weigh long-term expenses, comprehend hazards, and compare solutions. When making decisions, patience enables people to behave confidently rather than uncertainly.

Making the distinction between necessities and wants is another crucial component in making better decisions. Everyday living and future stability are supported by necessities like housing, food, transportation, healthcare, and education. Wants are not required to satisfy basic needs, but they do offer pleasure, comfort, or convenience. It is not necessary to discard pleasurable experiences in order to acknowledge this distinction. Rather, it promotes careful equilibrium. Making wise financial decisions entails fulfilling obligations while carefully weighing discretionary spending. People can enjoy their income without jeopardizing their future financial security thanks to this well-balanced method.

Making better financial decisions is mostly dependent on self-discipline. Advertising, social media, peer pressure, and easy access to finance are just a few of the various ways that temptation can manifest. These forces frequently promote emotional rather than thoughtful spending. Making it a practice to pause before making purchases gives you important time to think. Making smarter selections frequently results from asking straightforward questions about whether a purchase is required, economical, and consistent with long-term objectives. This pause promotes greater financial responsibility and lessens impulsive conduct.

Making better decisions can also be achieved by learning from past mistakes. At some point, everyone commits financial blunders. Budgets may occasionally be surpassed, investments may not perform as anticipated, or some purchases may turn out to be superfluous. Only when people honestly analyze these experiences and put the lessons learned into practice in the future do they become valuable. People who continuously make better financial decisions concentrate on comprehending what went wrong and coming up with better strategies for the future rather than wallowing in regret. Every error becomes a chance to improve financial savvy and sharpen judgment.

Effective emotion management is also essential to making better decisions. Financial conduct can be influenced by a variety of emotions, including fear, enthusiasm, irritation, envy, and overconfidence. Emotional judgments frequently ignore crucial information and result in behaviors that one may later regret. Someone might borrow money to keep up appearances, liquidate investments during brief market drops out of anxiety, or make an unnecessary purchase to reduce stress. Emotions must be balanced with careful consideration in order to make better financial decisions. Reflecting before making big decisions enables reason and long-term planning to take precedence over fleeting emotions.

Making better financial decisions is also facilitated by surrounding oneself with favorable influences. Through discussions and shared experiences, friends, family, coworkers, and mentors frequently influence attitudes toward money. Spending time with people who respect accountability, preparation, and personal development promotes better financial practices. Positive effects enhance deliberate decision-making and offer support in trying circumstances. Learning from seasoned professionals can assist steer clear of typical blunders while providing useful tactics that promote long-term success.

Acknowledging the opportunity cost of each financial move is another crucial concept. Money cannot be used for another purpose once it has been spent on one. This idea urges people to think about future chances that might be postponed in addition to the purchase's immediate worth. Spending money on pointless things can delay saving money, lowering debt, or making investments for future expansion. Comprehending opportunity cost promotes more deliberate spending as people start weighing options based on both current satisfaction and potential future outcomes.

Accepting accountability for financial results is another prerequisite for making better decisions. People still have control over many daily decisions, even as economic conditions, job possibilities, and unforeseen occurrences affect their budgets. Rather than blaming events beyond one's control, taking responsibility promotes proactive behavior. Individuals who concentrate on enhancing what they can control frequently make more progress since they focus their efforts on worthwhile endeavors, including developing new talents, enhancing budgeting, cutting back on wasteful spending, and preparing for upcoming obstacles.

In many facets of life, financial decision-making is strengthened by cultivating patience. Significant financial success seldom happens fast. It takes persistent effort over time to create investments, pay off debt, advance professionally, and save for crucial goals. People who are aware of this fact stay dedicated to steady advancement and steer clear of impractical promises of immediate achievement. Making sustainable decisions instead of taking quick cuts is frequently a better option. Patience lowers the possibility of needless risks while enabling financial strategies to develop.

Regular reflection also helps you make better decisions. Setting aside time to examine financial decisions offers beneficial chances to pinpoint areas of strength and development. People can assess their general financial habits, investment performance, savings development, and spending tendencies. Because each review provides insights that enhance future decisions, reflection promotes ongoing learning. Thoughtful people make changes that progressively improve their financial situation rather than continuing inefficient activities.

As better decisions become ingrained behaviors, confidence increases organically. Every prudent financial choice strengthens the conviction that discipline and preparation may lead to favorable results. Making wise choices, keeping savings, avoiding needless debt, and paying payments on time all contribute to a sense of control that lessens financial stress. People are motivated to keep improving because they are aware that their efforts yield significant outcomes. Because it reflects proven skill, confidence based on experience is more resilient than confidence based only on optimism.

Making better decisions affects various aspects of financial success in addition to money management. Long-term financial potential is impacted by decisions about relationships, education, professional development, health, and time management. Making the decision to learn new skills, keep up one's physical health, cultivate solid professional connections, and efficiently manage one's time frequently results in more income opportunities and enhances one's general quality of life. These more general life choices boost resilience, productivity, and individual efficacy, all of which contribute to financial prosperity.

Making better decisions ultimately comes down to cultivating an attitude that prioritizes deliberate decision-making over rash action. Every decision, no matter how minor, influences how someone's financial journey unfolds. Making decisions that advance long-term objectives on a regular basis generates momentum that improves financial stability and opens up new possibilities. Better decisions greatly raise the possibility of obtaining long-term stability and independence, but they do not remove obstacles or ensure instant success. People form habits that lead to better financial decisions at every stage of life through meticulous planning, ongoing education, emotional equilibrium, patience, and personal accountability. These decisions add up to significant advancements over time, proving that consistent decision-making that is in line with one's values, objectives, and future vision is the key to long-term financial success.

Small Changes Big Results

Since financial success is rarely defined by a few key decisions alone, one of the most significant abilities a person can acquire is the capacity to detect how money is spent on a daily basis. Rather, it is molded by hundreds of tiny decisions that frequently don't seem important enough. Even while a single pointless purchase might seem harmless, repeated purchases over weeks, months, and years have a subtle impact on debt, savings, investment prospects, and financial security. This chapter is important because it promotes awareness before money is lost rather than regret after it is gone. Consistent development is built by conscious action, which is the result of awareness. Every financial objective is dependent on everyday choices that either advance you toward your desired future or move you further away from it. Knowing where your money is going enables you to manage it purposefully rather than letting habits or feelings dictate where it ends up.

More than just spending habits are altered when the concepts discussed here are put into practice. It alters how you prioritize needs, assess value, and react to temptation. You start questioning if a purchase would help you achieve your greater financial goals rather than whether you can afford it. With this little change, money becomes a tool that supports your priorities rather than something that vanishes without a trace. Every financial decision you make becomes intentional rather than instinctive, which boosts your confidence. Savings start to increase as it becomes simpler to identify wasteful spending. Money is no longer secretly seeping into forgotten purchases, making debt reduction easier. With a better awareness of your financial patterns, planning becomes less stressful. Uncertainty gradually gives way to awareness, enabling every choice to contribute to increased stability and confidence.

Financial perplexity is frequently the result of disregarding these rules. Many people think they don't make enough money, but they've never really looked at how their money is being spent. Resources that may have increased savings or decreased debt are gradually consumed by little daily expenses, subscription renewals, impulsive purchases, convenience shopping, and emotional buying. These costs are simple to ignore until financial strain becomes unbearable since they happen gradually. The lack of funds for planning makes handling unforeseen catastrophes more challenging. Financial objectives stay far off because steady advancement never occurs. Because there is no obvious reason why money seems to vanish every month, stress levels rise. Even when income rises, the lack of awareness frequently leads to frustration because spending patterns don't change.

Increasing spending intentionality has a real-world impact on all facets of daily life. People feel more at ease because they know exactly where their money is going. Financial priorities become apparent and shared, which improves family communication. Because spending decisions are made based on predetermined goals rather than impulse, couples have fewer arguments. Youngsters see responsible financial behavior that is modeled for them on a daily basis. When resources are allocated to worthwhile goals rather than fleeting enjoyment, long-term objectives become more attainable. Financial confidence increases when decisions are more deliberate and consistent with personal ideals rather than when every obstacle vanishes.

By the end of this chapter, you will be able to recognize spending patterns that either improve or worsen your financial future, make deliberate purchases that support your long-term goals rather than fleeting emotions, and establish regular daily routines that boost your financial confidence and increase your chances for investing, saving, and prudent money management.

Think about Anthony's experience, who frequently questioned why he had trouble saving money even though he was getting regular pay raises. He thought that unforeseen costs were to blame, although he never looked closely at his daily expenditures. He found dozens of little expenses that had become routine after keeping track of every purchase for a month. A sizable amount of his salary was being discreetly consumed by impulsive internet purchases, regular food deliveries, digital subscriptions he hardly ever used, and morning coffee he bought on the way to work. Anthony chose the least valuable expenses rather than getting rid of all the fun ones. He implemented a 24-hour waiting period before making non-essential purchases, canceled unwanted subscriptions, and made coffee at home several mornings a week. Every month, his savings were automatically deposited into an investment account. He had amassed significantly more than he had anticipated in just one year. The most important lesson was not how much he saved, but rather how effective minor adjustments could be when made repeatedly.

The same truth is illustrated by a simple anecdote. Two identical flower beds were maintained by an old gardener. He pulled a few weeds from the first bed each morning, but he ignored the second since the weeds there appeared insignificant. After a few weeks, the neglected bed grew overgrown, making it challenging for healthy flowers to get nutrition and sunlight. Because minor issues had been resolved before they grew into major ones, the well-maintained bed prospered. The development of financial habits is similar. Tiny unneeded expenses are like little weeds. They steadily deplete resources and restrict growth when left unchecked. When properly handled, they foster sound financial practices and yield long-term benefits.

The steering wheel of a car serves as a helpful metaphor for everyday financial decisions. Even a small alteration can result in a completely different destination over a lengthy voyage, even though it may seem minor at the time. Every expenditure choice operates in the same manner. Even though a single purchase might seem insignificant, repeated decisions eventually steer your financial life in the direction of stability or hardship. Unnoticed habits gradually pull you away from your objectives, yet small adjustments made consistently keep you heading in the right direction. The steering wheel serves as a reminder that direction is frequently more crucial than speed, as it ultimately dictates our destination.

Use the Pause Review Decide Framework to start putting these concepts into practice right away. Start by taking a moment before making any unnecessary purchases rather than acting on convenience or emotion right away. Make sure you have adequate room to think about whether the purchase is really necessary. Next, consider whether the expense aligns with your values, present priorities, or long-term financial goals. Think about other, more affordable, or more valuable ways to satisfy the same demand. Make a deliberate choice rather than an impulsive one after thoroughly considering your options. If the purchase is still worthwhile, move forward guilt-free and with confidence as it fits with your priorities. If it doesn't help you achieve your objectives, move the funds to future investments, debt reduction, or savings. Continue doing this until making deliberate decisions rather than impulsive purchases comes naturally to you.

This framework's simplicity is what makes it strong. Perfection or total constraint are not necessary. Rather, it promotes awareness prior to action. Eliminating every pleasurable spending is rarely the path to financial prosperity. Instead, it is accomplished by making sure that expenditures represent real priorities rather than ingrained behaviors. You can continue to build long-term security while enjoying your money thanks to this balanced approach. Every deliberate choice you make builds self-control and the conviction that you are in charge of your finances rather than letting them rule you.

The odd dramatic effort is still considerably less desirable than consistency. Many people try rigorous financial adjustments for a little time before giving up since the strategy seems unfeasible. Manageable advancements that can be sustained over time lead to sustainable progress. Individually, decisions like bringing lunch from home twice a week, cooking more frequently, cutting back on pointless subscriptions, comparing prices before making significant purchases, or postponing impulsive purchases by one day might seem tiny. But when combined, these practices result in significant financial gains over a number of years. Extreme sacrifice rarely results in long-term wealth. It is developed by making deliberate choices on a regular basis that become ingrained in daily life.

It's also critical to realize that awareness should never lead to guilt. Examining spending is done to make better judgments in the future, not to point out previous errors. Everybody has made purchases that they later questioned. Only when such experiences lead to better decisions in the future do they become worthwhile. When action and knowledge are joined, progress starts. Instead of letting old patterns dictate your future, each day offers you another chance to allocate your finances to the things that really matter.

As you become more conscious, you could also see how emotions affect financial choices. If unchecked, stress, boredom, enthusiasm, celebration, and disappointment can all lead to wasteful expenditure. You can replace instinctive behaviors with deliberate ones by identifying these emotional triggers. You start utilizing financial discipline to establish long-lasting peace of mind rather than using money to ease transient feelings. Because it increases careful planning and decreases impulsive conduct, this emotional awareness reinforces all other financial habits.

Consider whether your daily expenditures represent your most important goals or your fleeting feelings. Which ongoing expense costs the most money over time yet offers the least value? Which one of your spending habits could you change this week to help your finances in the future? How may being more conscious of your everyday financial decisions enhance your relationships, self-esteem, and prospects for the future? What tiny choice can you make now that you will value in the future?

One flawless choice never results in significant financial advancement. It is the result of innumerable deliberate decisions made repeatedly throughout time. The future you are building is strengthened by each deliberate purchase, each avoidable spend, and each dollar spent on worthwhile objectives. Keep putting these ideas into practice with perseverance and assurance, understanding that even modest advancements add up to amazing outcomes. The route to long-term financial success is shaped by daily choices that demonstrate insight, purpose, and consistency rather than by sporadic acts of discipline. Continue making those choices, day by day, and let every minor advancement turn into a long-term move toward more financial independence and peace of mind.

CHAPTER IV

Smart Budget Planning

Building Practical Budget

Creating a sensible budget is one of the best ways to build long-term wealth and financial stability. A budget is not intended to limit freedom or take away fun from life. Rather, it acts as a guide to assist people in allocating their financial resources to the most important priorities and objectives. Money frequently vanishes in the absence of a sensible budget due to impulsive choices, unforeseen bills, and unplanned spending. Many people put forth a lot of effort to make a living, yet they still struggle financially because they don't have a clear strategy for handling their earnings. Income is transformed into a useful tool by a well-designed budget, supporting current requirements while setting the stage for future opportunities.

A thorough grasp of revenue is the first step in creating a practical budget. To ensure that financial decisions are founded on precise knowledge rather than conjecture, every source of funding should be specified. Employment, self-employment, investments, rental properties, and other dependable sources can all generate income. Every other budgetary decision is based on the precise amount of money that enters the family each month. People benefit from making conservative projections based on average earnings when their income changes in order to prepare for times when it may temporarily fall. An honest assessment of the resources at hand discourages irrational spending plans and promotes prudent money management.

Finding every regular expense is the next step. Housing, utilities, insurance, loan payments, transportation, and communication services are examples of fixed costs that usually don't change every month. Depending on individual preferences and situations, variable costs including groceries, fuel, entertainment, clothing, eating, and personal care may vary. A comprehensive picture of financial commitments and chances for improvement can be obtained by listing every expense. Because these transactions seem tiny on their own, many consumers underestimate how much they spend on smaller purchases. When taken as a whole, nevertheless, they frequently account for considerable amounts of monthly income.

Instead of reflecting irrational expectations, a practical budget represents reality. Making an ideal budget while ignoring real spending patterns and everyday obligations is a common error. Because they necessitate significant lifestyle adjustments, budgets that demand instant perfection are sometimes hard to stick to. Instead, by making reasonable changes that can be maintained over time, effective budgeting promotes incremental improvement. When people's financial goals take into account their existing situation while gradually adopting healthier behaviors, they are more likely to stay committed.

Another crucial element of a sensible budget is flexibility. Unexpected events like medical bills, auto repairs, house upkeep, family emergencies, or brief fluctuations in income are all part of life. When circumstances change, a strict budget that does not allow for modifications frequently leads to frustration. Setting up money for unforeseen costs lowers stress and keeps long-term financial advancement from being hampered by crises. Budgets that are flexible can change without compromising overall financial objectives.

Setting priorities for necessities is a key component of efficient budgeting. The basis for financial stability is provided by housing, food, healthcare, utilities, transportation, and required insurance. Prior to distributing funds for discretionary spending, fulfilling these tasks guarantees that fundamental duties are regularly carried out. The money left over after basic necessities are met might be used for investments, savings, debt repayment, personal growth, leisure, and other worthwhile objectives. Setting priorities boosts confidence in day-to-day decision-making while lowering financial uncertainty.

Instead of being a sporadic activity done just when additional money is available, saving should be viewed as a regular financial obligation. Many people want to save whatever is left over after purchasing, yet this strategy frequently yields little to no progress because unforeseen expenditures deplete available funds. Planned savings are a necessary expense from the start in a practical budget. Even little donations done regularly over a long period of time can increase dramatically while bolstering financial stability and lowering reliance on debt in times of need.

Another crucial component of a sensible budget is debt management. Monthly budgeting should properly account for loan payments, credit card balances, and other financial commitments. By creating a budget, people can keep an eye on their repayment progress and try to avoid taking on more debt. By releasing revenue that can subsequently support savings, investments, or other financial priorities, debt reduction progressively increases cash flow. Increased financial flexibility and more opportunities in the future are represented by each payment made toward debt elimination.

Identifying one's own spending patterns is another necessary step in creating a sensible budget. Emotions, rituals, family experiences, advertising, and social expectations all have an impact on each person's distinct financial behaviors. Examining historical expenditure trends makes it easier to spot places where funds might be slipping out of the budget without contributing to worthwhile objectives. People frequently find ongoing costs that have little long-term worth. By identifying these trends, resources can be rerouted to objectives that increase long-term happiness and financial stability.

Budgeting decisions are strengthened when needs and wants are distinguished. While wants improve comfort, enjoyment, or convenience, essential requirements sustain day-to-day existence and individual well-being. Both categories are valuable, but carefully weighing them can help avoid needless financial strain. A sensible budget guarantees that discretionary expenditure does not conflict with long-term goals while allowing for enjoyment. Eliminating pleasure activities entirely frequently leads to frustration and makes maintaining the budget challenging. Healthy financial practices that are long-lasting are encouraged by moderation.

Maintaining a budget is motivated by well-defined financial goals. An organized financial plan makes it easier to save for a home, pay off debt, create an emergency fund, invest for retirement, launch a business, or pay for college. Every budgetary choice becomes more meaningful when it is linked to certain personal goals. When people realize that every financial decision they make adds to a more fulfilling future, they are more inclined to put off fleeting pleasures.

Maintaining an efficient budget requires regular assessment. Over time, personal priorities, family obligations, income, and expenses all inevitably shift. People may compare planned and actual spending while identifying areas that need to be adjusted thanks to monthly evaluations. Learning should take precedence over criticism in these reviews. Every budgeting experience yields insightful data that enhances subsequent financial choices. Consistently making little improvements often yields better long-term outcomes than making large changes infrequently.

Budgeting is now easier than ever thanks to technology. Financial tracking is made easier and more accurate with the use of digital banking, budgeting software, online account access, and electronic payment records. However, a budget's efficacy is more dependent on how consistently it is applied than on the particular techniques used. Regular attention is still essential for effective financial management, whether digital solutions or conventional printed records are used.

The budgeting process can be considerably strengthened by family involvement. When all parties are aware of common objectives and take part in responsible decision-making, financial plans are more successful. While lowering misconceptions around expenditure priorities, open communication promotes cooperation. When parents engage their kids in age-appropriate financial conversations, they also help them acquire important money management skills that will benefit future generations. Budgeting turns into a chance to improve collaboration and shared accountability in addition to being a financial endeavor.

Since significant financial improvement seldom occurs right away, patience is required. It takes effort, self-control, and consistent practice to develop sound budgeting practices. Periodic setbacks should be seen as chances to enhance future planning rather than as failures. When people stay dedicated to their financial objectives, unforeseen costs, shifting conditions, or brief overspending do not undo long-term gains. In the end, consistency over months and years yields significantly better results than trying to find quick fixes or make significant short-term adjustments.

Increased peace of mind is another benefit of a sensible budget. Because people are unclear about their ability to fulfill future obligations, financial uncertainty frequently results in needless stress. It gives confidence in both routine situations and unforeseen obstacles to know that money has been carefully distributed toward savings, debt reduction, critical necessities, and meaningful priorities. Instead of responding emotionally to shifting circumstances, this sense of control enables people to make financial decisions with more clarity.

Constructing congruence between financial resources and personal beliefs is ultimately the key to constructing a practical budget. Every dollar earned is a chance to support the life one aspires to. A well-considered budget turns money from something that comes and goes into a potent instrument for accomplishing important objectives. People can create financial habits that support long-term stability and prosperity by analyzing their income, managing their expenses, saving consistently, controlling debt, monitoring their progress on a regular basis, and being adaptable when things change. A functional budget eventually evolves beyond a monthly financial plan. It turns into a daily manual that promotes prudent choices, boosts self-esteem, safeguards upcoming opportunities, and builds a strong basis for long-term financial success.

Managing Monthly Cash

Effective monthly cash management defines how income is used to fulfill current requirements while preparing for future opportunities, making it one of the most crucial skills for attaining long-term financial stability. Financial success is contingent upon the prudent management of available funds throughout each month, regardless of an individual's income. Many people think that having a higher income will instantly fix their financial issues, but without smart preparation, even large earnings can soon vanish. On the other hand, people with small earnings frequently develop financial security through regular, purposeful, and disciplined money management. Through deliberate daily choices, effective cash management enables people to fulfill their responsibilities, lower financial stress, boost savings, and progressively accumulate long-term wealth.

Knowing how much money is left over after taxes and other deductions is the first step in managing your monthly finances. The actual resources available for spending, savings, investments, and personal objectives are represented by this sum. When people spend based on what they anticipate earning rather than what they actually receive, many financial problems result. A sound basis for responsible planning is established by a realistic assessment of available revenue. It is simpler to allocate money wisely and prevent needless financial strain when one is aware of the precise amount of money that enters the household each month.

Knowing where your money goes each month is equally important. Small everyday purchases can add up to large sums, so many people are shocked when they carefully examine their expenditures. Essential financial obligations include regular costs, including rent, utilities, transportation, groceries, insurance, medical care, and communication services. Discretionary costs like entertainment, eating out, hobbies, subscriptions, and impulsive purchases go hand in hand with these. Monitoring both areas helps find ways to increase cash flow without compromising general quality of life and offers insightful information about spending patterns.

One of the most useful strategies for efficient money management is to make a monthly spending plan. Every part of income is given a purpose by a spending plan before it is spent. At the end of the month, people actively choose how resources will be spent rather than wondering where their money went. Priority is given to necessities, then savings, debt reduction, investments, and leisure. This strategy lessens the possibility of overspending and promotes deliberate decision-making. A well-thought-out spending plan allows people to enjoy their income while keeping their finances in balance by acting as guidance rather than a limitation.

Differentiating between fixed and variable expenses is another aspect of managing monthly cash. Rent, mortgage payments, insurance premiums, and loan payments are examples of fixed expenses that often stay the same each month. Groceries, transit costs, entertainment, and utility bills are examples of variable expenses that vary based on circumstances and lifestyle choices. Knowing these distinctions enables people to pinpoint locations where essential improvements can be made. Reducing discretionary expenditure frequently offers flexibility during financially difficult months without compromising important obligations.

Paying critical debts first is a crucial cash management practice. The necessities of daily life—housing, food, healthcare, transportation, and utilities—should take precedence over optional expenditures. Consistently fulfilling these obligations safeguards long-term stability and avoids needless financial strain. The money left over after paying for necessities can be used for investments, debt repayment, savings, and well-planned discretionary spending. This hierarchy of priorities helps avoid circumstances in which money has already been spent elsewhere, making it difficult to pay crucial expenses.

Another crucial element of monthly money management is regular saving. Many people put off saving what's left until the end of the month, but this strategy frequently yields little to no savings since unforeseen costs and impulsive expenditures deplete available funds. More consistency is encouraged when savings are viewed as a regular financial obligation. Setting aside a percentage of income as soon as it is received improves financial discipline and progressively accumulates funds for important life objectives, future investments, and emergencies. When contributions are provided consistently over extended periods of time, even small ones gain significance.

Preparing for sporadic expenses that arise during the year is another aspect of managing monthly cash. Many financial difficulties are caused by infrequent rather than unexpected expenses. When unanticipated, annual insurance premiums, holiday celebrations, school bills, home maintenance, auto repairs, and medical charges, frequently cause financial difficulty. The cost is spread out over time, and unexpected financial strain is avoided by setting aside a modest sum each month for these predictable occurrences. When these costs come up, preparation boosts confidence and lessens the need for borrowing.

Avoiding needless debt is another important part of cash management. When used properly, borrowing can be helpful for large purchases like home ownership or school. However, using credit to pay for regular monthly needs frequently results in long-term financial problems. Interest charges lower future financial flexibility and raise the overall cost of purchases. Carefully managing monthly funds enables people to live within their means, enhancing their financial independence and lowering reliance on borrowing.

Another crucial element of efficient money management is flexibility. Monthly spending plans should be adjusted to reflect changing life situations. Prices may go up, family needs may change, income may go up or down, or new opportunities may present themselves. Regularly reviewing financial plans enables people to make deliberate changes while staying dedicated to long-term objectives. Being flexible doesn't imply giving up on financial discipline; rather, it means reacting appropriately to shifting conditions without losing sight of the big picture.

Controlling impulsive spending is another essential component of efficient monthly cash management. Purchasing goods and services is now easier than ever thanks to modern technology, which frequently encourages snap judgments without critical thought. Promotional deals, social media, and advertising often put pressure on consumers to overspend. People can assess if a purchase aligns with their financial priorities by forming the practice of delaying purchases. This little period of introspection frequently stops wasteful spending and frees up funds for more worthwhile endeavors.

When handling household finances with family members, communication becomes even more crucial. More understanding and collaboration result from candid conversations about income, expenses, financial objectives, and spending preferences. Financially responsible family members benefit from setting shared goals and encouraging one another to make wise choices. Clear communication encourages everyone to contribute to shared financial success, enhances accountability, and minimizes misunderstandings.

Keeping an eye on cash flow throughout the month offers important chances to make changes before issues arise. If you wait until the end of the month to assess your finances, you can find overspending when there aren't many ways to make it right. Frequent evaluations help people stay in line with their financial objectives, spot patterns early, and modify discretionary spending as needed. Regular check-ins improve awareness and promote proactive decision-making as opposed to reactive reactions to financial difficulties.

By lowering financial uncertainty, monthly cash management also promotes mental well-being. Uncertainty about having enough money to fulfill future responsibilities causes stress for a lot of people. Clarity regarding available resources, impending costs, and financial progress is provided by a well-organized cash management system. Because they are more aware of their financial situation, people feel less anxious and more confident. One of the most important advantages of prudent money management is peace of mind.

The capacity to take advantage of opportunities is a significant benefit of efficient monthly cash management. Financial flexibility enables people to take advantage of possibilities when they present themselves, whether they are investing in potential chances, starting a business, seeking further education, or managing unforeseen travel or family demands. These possibilities could be lost if cash management isn't done carefully because money is already being spent on wasteful spending or excessive debt. Making prudent financial decisions opens up new opportunities.

It takes perseverance and consistency, not perfection, to form this habit. Careful planning may be more challenging in certain months due to unforeseen costs or financial setbacks. Continued effort should not be discouraged by these encounters. Rather, they offer valuable insights that enhance future planning. Every month presents a fresh chance to improve financial practices, make better spending choices, and get closer to long-term financial objectives. Periods of flawless financial management interspersed with negligence are significantly less useful than continuous development.

In the end, monthly cash management is about allocating financial resources purposefully rather than letting events or impulses dictate spending. Every dollar received is a chance to improve one's financial security, uphold one's moral principles, and get ready for success in the future. People have more control over their finances and build a stronger foundation for long-term prosperity through cautious planning, deliberate spending, consistent saving, frequent evaluation, and responsible decision-making. This methodical strategy gradually turns monthly income into a potent weapon for attaining financial security, lowering needless stress, increasing prospects for the future, and creating a life driven by deliberate decisions rather than financial uncertainty. Regular monthly cash management shows that wise monthly administration of available resources determines long-term prosperity rather than just income.

Adjusting Financial Plans

Since life is ever-changing, making adjustments to financial plans is crucial to creating long-term prosperity. A financial plan should never be thought of as something that is made once and then adhered to without change. Rather, it ought to serve as an adaptable manual that changes in tandem with individual circumstances, financial objectives, family obligations, professional prospects, and economic situations. Even the most meticulously crafted strategy is unable to foresee every event that will take place over a long period of time. People who see the value of making deliberate changes are better equipped to safeguard their financial security while pursuing long-term success. They perceive change as a necessary component of sound financial management rather than as a setback.

The shifting nature of revenue is one of the main reasons financial plans need to be adjusted. Throughout their lives, many people encounter pay rises, promotions, profession shifts, business expansion, or brief drops in income. Every one of these circumstances brings with it new possibilities and obligations. People have the opportunity to raise savings, speed up debt repayment, increase investments, or get ready for future goals when their income rises. Higher income, however, might result in increased expenditure if the financial strategy isn't modified. Despite increasing income, this pattern—often referred to as lifestyle inflation—can impede significant financial advancement. It is easier to make sure that extra income supports long-term priorities rather than wasteful spending when financial plans are updated in response to changes in income.

Financial adjustments may also be required due to unforeseen life circumstances. Even the most meticulously planned budget can be severely impacted by medical emergencies, family responsibilities, house repairs, auto upkeep, or brief unemployment. Even while emergency savings lessen the effects of these circumstances, financial plans could still need to be modified to account for shifting priorities. People may have to put off some aspirations during difficult times in order to safeguard their vital financial obligations. By carefully making these changes, people can preserve stability without giving up on their long-term goals.

Financial planning decisions are influenced by the natural evolution of family circumstances over time. Income requirements and spending priorities are impacted by a number of factors, including marriage, the birth of children, educational costs, taking care of aging parents, and changes in household size. Financial strategies should take these new realities into account as obligations increase. Retirement planning, housing choices, savings objectives, and insurance coverage may all need to be adjusted to accommodate evolving family demands. Reviewing financial priorities on a regular basis guarantees that the people and tasks that are most important continue to receive the resources that are available.

Financial planning is also influenced by career progression. At various phases of life, people frequently seek further education, professional certifications, career changes, or entrepreneurial chances. While some of these choices offer chances for future economic growth and personal fulfillment, they also necessitate short-term financial compromises. By modifying their financial plans, people can get ready for these changes without needless financial strain. Maintaining stability while investing in long-term career advancement is made easier by making plans for short-term changes in income or higher school costs.

Another significant aspect that needs regular financial changes is inflation. The price of housing, food, transportation, healthcare, education, and daily needs progressively rises with time. When expenses continue to climb but purchasing power decreases, a financial strategy that is left unaltered for many years may become ineffective. Regular budget reviews enable people to keep moving closer to their financial objectives while taking pricing changes into consideration. Gradual adjustments are frequently easier to handle than waiting until financial strain becomes unbearable.

As people mature and acquire new experiences, their financial objectives often shift. At first, a young professional might concentrate on saving for emergencies, paying off student loans, or buying their first house. Later on, priorities could change to include starting a business, growing investments, raising children, or getting ready for retirement. Financial strategies should take these shifting goals into account as life changes. Regularly reviewing goals ensures that everyday financial decisions stay relevant to current priorities rather than out-of-date goals that don't fit individual circumstances.

Periodic evaluation and modification of investment strategy is also advantageous. People's tolerance for financial risk frequently shifts as they get closer to different life stages. While those who are getting close to retirement might place a higher priority on stability and income preservation, younger investors might select portfolios that emphasize long-term gain. Investment decisions are also influenced by market conditions, but modifications should always be based on careful planning rather than impulsive responses to transient swings. Long-term financial security is supported by keeping a diversified investment plan and routinely assessing results.

Plans for managing debt may also need to be updated over time. Some people have the chance to pay off debt faster because they make more money or spend less. Others could require short-term modifications due to unforeseen financial commitments. People might assess whether new payments, refinancing options, or adjusted repayment plans better suit their overall financial objectives by reviewing debt repayment strategies. Maintaining momentum without compromising crucial financial stability is made possible by flexibility.

A sincere assessment of one's own spending patterns is also necessary for modifying financial strategies. Spending habits naturally shift in tandem with changes in income, family obligations, and personal interests. Frequent reviews assist in identifying costs that are no longer in line with the priorities of the present. Certain expenditures that were once worthwhile might no longer be necessary, and new objectives can call for more funding. Careful analysis promotes deliberate spending as opposed to letting antiquated behaviors persist on their own.

Keeping an eye on financial development yields important knowledge that directs wise changes. People can assess if their current techniques are yielding the expected outcomes by keeping track of their savings balances, debt reduction, investment growth, and monthly expenses. Adjustments can be made before serious issues arise if financial goals seem unattainable or progress slows. Financial planning becomes an active system of continual improvement when progress is measured.

When making changes to financial plans, emotional resilience is crucial. Many people lose hope when unforeseen circumstances force them to alter well-planned objectives. Flexibility, however, should never be seen as a sign of failure. Effective money management acknowledges that one of the best qualities people can cultivate is flexibility. Maintaining focus on long-term goals while making the required short-term adjustments shows maturity and wisdom rather than weakness. Financial success is judged by how well one responds to changing circumstances rather than by avoiding every obstacle.

When financial decisions have an impact on several family members, open communication is extremely crucial. Reviewing financial success, talking about shifting priorities, and working together to make adjustments are all beneficial for couples and families. While ensuring that everyone is aware of common objectives and duties, open dialogue fosters trust. In both successful and difficult times, collaborative planning minimizes miscommunication and promotes teamwork.

Successful financial changes are also supported by keeping reasonable expectations. Many individuals assume that financial advancement will happen in a straight line, but this is rarely the case in real life. Financial results are influenced by a variety of factors, including shifts in income, the state of the economy, individual obligations, and unforeseen opportunities. Instead of getting disheartened by brief setbacks, people can stay patient and dedicated by realizing that adjustments are a typical part of the trip.

The capacity to make prudent financial plan adjustments is further strengthened by ongoing education. Reading, educational courses, expert guidance, and real-world experience all contribute to the expansion of financial knowledge. People are better able to hone their financial strategy when they learn more about long-term planning, investing, taxes, insurance, and budgeting. When crucial financial decisions are made, learning promotes confidence while lowering uncertainty.

Regularly reviewing financial planning promotes consistency and keeps minor problems from growing into major ones. Annual goal assessments, quarterly financial evaluations, and monthly budget reviews offer organized chances to monitor progress and make deliberate changes. These frequent evaluations enable people to stay focused on their financial goals while proactively responding to evolving situations rather than waiting until problems arise.

In the end, modifying financial plans is about safeguarding objectives rather than giving up on them. Flexibility enables people to focus on long-term financial achievement while adapting successfully to changing circumstances. Every change offers a chance to better align one's values, resources, and goals for the future. People can increase their capacity to accumulate long-term wealth over time by continuing to make deliberate financial decisions, staying flexible, regularly assessing their progress, and wisely reacting to life's changes. The best financial plans are those that change with the individuals they are intended to assist, offering direction at every stage of life and fostering stability, resiliency, and significant financial development.

Strength Through Consistency

The recurring decisions that mold daily living affect financial success rather than sporadic acts of self-control. Many people enthusiastically draft a financial plan, only to give up on it within a few weeks due to unforeseen costs, shifting priorities, or just plain despair. Applying a sensible financial plan regularly over time is what gives it its genuine value. This chapter is important because it shows that sustaining consistent routines rather than aiming for flawless performance leads to long-term financial security. Only when a well-thought-out strategy is consistently applied to support long-term goals, guide decisions, and adjust to changing conditions does it become significant. Financial planning becomes a dependable lifestyle that boosts confidence, lowers uncertainty, and fortifies all future decisions when it is done consistently.

By putting the ideas discussed in this chapter into practice, people's everyday financial practices are altered. They start responding to every financial circumstance with preparedness and purpose rather than emotionally. Before being spent, monthly income is clearly directed. Instead of being unpleasant surprises, necessary expenses are anticipated. Instead of being a sporadic leftover, savings become a regular goal. The deliberate allocation of available resources makes debt repayment more structured. When expectations are discussed and understood, family financial conversations become more fruitful. Over time, these regular practices foster a sense of control that goes beyond money. Every month offers another chance to reinforce good habits that promote future stability, and confidence increases as progress becomes apparent.

Financial frustration frequently results from ignoring these teachings. Money tends to vanish inexplicably in the absence of a trustworthy strategy, making it challenging to comprehend why financial objectives continue to elude achievement. Despite a rise in income, financial strain persists due to aimless expenditure. Due to inadequate planning, unforeseen costs become overwhelming. Small financial issues build up to major stress, which frequently has an impact on relationships, productivity at work, and emotional health. Many people wrongly think they don't have the means to better their circumstances, but inconsistency—rather than income—is the bigger obstacle. An often-abandoned plan cannot yield long-term outcomes. Lack of sound financial practices frequently results in uncertainty, lost opportunities, and needless reliance on credit during trying times.

In both typical and exceptional situations, the practical benefits of upholding sound financial practices become apparent. Because regular planning lessens uncertainty about monthly obligations, families feel more at ease. Because they know exactly where their money is going, people feel more comfortable making financial decisions. Because emergency savings offer more flexibility during times of upheaval, career prospects become easier to seek. Because preparedness has taken the place of fear, unforeseen repairs or medical costs become doable. When consistent progress is made month after month, long-term goals like home ownership, education, travel, or retirement become attainable. The biggest advantage is not just cash gain but also the assurance that your everyday choices are building a better future.

By the end of this chapter, you will be able to develop disciplined habits that strengthen savings, improve financial stability, and lessen needless financial stress through consistent and deliberate action. You will also be able to establish a practical financial routine that supports consistent monthly progress and confidently modify your financial plan when life circumstances change without losing sight of your long-term priorities.

Take Elaine's experience, who frequently had big financial objectives at the start of each year but seldom adhered to them for longer than a month. She gave up on her entire plan and reverted to her previous spending patterns once unforeseen costs arose. She eventually took a more straightforward stance. She concentrated on examining her finances every Sunday night rather than striving for perfection. She evaluated her expenditures against her monthly budget, made any required adjustments for impending costs, and acknowledged even minor gains. She saw rare setbacks as chances to get better rather than as reasons to give up. She steadily paid off debt, saved more money, and created an emergency fund over the course of the next two years, which boosted her confidence. She didn't make significant sacrifices to achieve financial success. It resulted from sticking to a straightforward schedule that she could reliably adhere to in spite of shifting conditions.

This idea is aptly demonstrated in a short narrative. A stone mason was questioned about how he built a wonderful structure that had endured for many centuries. Assuming the endeavor required incredible moments of effort, visitors marveled at the striking walls and exquisite design. The mason grinned and stated that the edifice was made possible by his meticulous daily placement of one stone at a time without sacrificing the caliber of his work. On some days, the building's progress was nearly undetectable, but each stone that was positioned correctly strengthened the structure until it was finished. The development of financial prosperity follows a similar pattern. Repeated daily decisions that may seem routine at the time but become extraordinary over time are what generate long-lasting stability.

The constant rhythm of a heartbeat serves as a helpful metaphor for financial discipline. Strong beats interspersed with extended quiet intervals are not necessary for a healthy heart. Rather, it runs on a steady, consistent beat that keeps life going throughout the day. The same is true of financial habits. Months of neglect cannot be made up for by a single month of flawless budgeting. Similarly, years of disciplined habits are not destroyed by a single financial setback. The strength is in keeping a steady pace of deliberate choices. Over the course of a lifetime, financial health is strengthened by a dependable pattern that is created by each consistent activity supporting the next.

Use the Review Adjust Continue Framework to start putting these concepts into practice right away. Start by evaluating your financial status once a week or once a month. Analyze your earnings, outlays, savings, and advancement toward your financial goals without passing judgment. Next, modify your plan to reflect the current situation. If unforeseen costs occur, adjust less crucial expenditures rather than giving up on your entire plan. Before the next review period, identify one improvement that can be made. Then, realizing that consistency is more important than perfection, carry out your strategy with renewed dedication. To make financial planning a normal habit rather than an infrequent occurrence, repeat this cycle on a regular basis. This straightforward architecture maintains long-term direction while gradually fostering flexibility.

This framework's strength stems from its capacity to adapt to real-world situations. Plans for finances should never be so inflexible that they break down when conditions change. Careful modifications are necessary due to unforeseen costs, income fluctuations, family obligations, or new opportunities. You can react sensibly while staying dedicated to your bigger financial goals when you have a flexible plan. Repeating the same acts in the face of shifting circumstances is not what is meant by consistency. It entails being true to your goals while making required adjustments to your approach.

Realizing that minor advancements merit acknowledgment is another crucial lesson. Instead of enjoying quantifiable progress, many people feel disheartened by comparing their current circumstances with far-off ambitions. Meaningful accomplishments include paying off a single debt, somewhat boosting savings, cutting back on wasteful spending, or finishing another month of prudent money management. Celebrating these accomplishments promotes sustained effort and strengthens the conviction that long-term success is already emerging. Evidence builds confidence, and each step that is accomplished shows that constructive change is occurring.

Because recurring behaviors lessen emotional reactivity, consistency also improves decision-making. You start depending on established patterns that encourage deliberate action rather than making financial decisions based on fleeting enthusiasm, fear, or pressure. This methodical technique keeps you safe in both good and bad times. Consistency keeps reckless spending at bay during prosperous times. It offers direction and stability during difficult times, which lowers stress and promotes sensible changes rather than rash decisions.

It's equally vital to keep in mind that speed isn't necessarily the best indicator of development. While some months will see quick progress, others might maintain stability in the face of unforeseen difficulties. Both results are worthwhile. Maintaining good habits during challenging times frequently shows more resilience than making quick gains when things are going well. Patience enables persistent efforts to yield outcomes that might not be apparent right away but grow in importance over time.

Consider whether your present financial regimen relies on sporadic motivation or promotes long-term growth. With just a minor change to your daily routine, which financial behavior could become more consistent? When unforeseen costs interfere with your financial plans, how do you typically react? What routine review procedure could you employ to stay on top of your priorities every month? If you regularly adhered to a straightforward and sustainable financial plan each week, how would your future financial confidence improve?

Every long-term financial success is the result of consistent dedication rather than overt effort. The opportunities you have tomorrow will be shaped by the behaviors you choose to maintain today. By accepting constancy as your greatest asset, you may continue to fortify your financial future. Give yourself permission to reinforce the life you are purposefully constructing with each review, deliberate modification, and disciplined choice. Perfection is not necessary for progress. It calls for perseverance, tolerance, and the determination to keep going in spite of brief obstacles. Every steady step you take will serve as a strong foundation for a future characterized by assurance, stability, opportunity, and long-term financial success if you stay true to these ideals.

CHAPTER V

Saving With Purpose

Emergency Fund Growth

One of the best financial defenses a person can develop is an emergency fund, which offers security against unforeseen circumstances that may otherwise result in severe financial difficulty. There are many unknowns in life that are not always foreseeable or avoidable. Unexpected events include medical costs, job loss, auto repairs, house maintenance, family emergencies, or brief income decreases. Even though these circumstances are frequently inevitable, keeping an emergency fund can significantly lessen the financial effect. It takes more than just amassing money to build and expand this financial reserve. It is about developing steadiness, self-assurance, and the capacity to react composedly to unforeseen difficulties.

Many people erroneously think that persons with significant financial risks or erratic incomes are the only ones who need emergency funds. In actuality, everyone may profit from setting away money for unanticipated expenses. Even those with stable jobs, reliable businesses, or multiple sources of income may encounter unforeseen circumstances that momentarily impact their financial status. As a personal financial safety net, an emergency fund offers quick access to resources without the need for credit cards, personal loans, or outside help. This independence lessens needless stress during trying times and improves financial security.

Understanding the objective of an emergency fund is the first step towards growing it. The funds are not meant for scheduled expenses, entertainment, luxury items, or trips. Rather, it is specifically designed to deal with real circumstances that call for quick financial assistance. Its intended function is preserved when emergency funds are kept apart from ordinary spending accounts. People are less likely to use these funds for unnecessary expenditures when they have a clear definition of what constitutes an emergency. This discipline guarantees that the reserve will be accessible when it is really needed.

Consistency is one of the key tenets of emergency fund growth. Many people put off saving because they think significant improvement won't be possible unless they make significant contributions. However, making modest but consistent payments is typically the first step in creating financial security. Over time, consistent growth is produced by setting aside a small sum each week or month. Contributions may progressively increase as income rises or costs fall. Because it fosters long-term financial discipline that supports numerous other financial objectives, the habit of regular saving is frequently more useful than the amount of any one deposit.

Long-term success is greatly enhanced by making emergency savings a regular monthly priority. People gain from saving away money as soon as they receive income rather than waiting to save what's left over after spending. This strategy supports the notion that conserving money is a necessary financial obligation rather than a choice. Giving emergency savings a permanent spot in the monthly budget allows people to accumulate a reserve without feeling overburdened by the process progressively. Even modest donations over time result in significant financial protection.

Growing an emergency savings account requires patience. It takes time to accumulate a sizeable financial reserve, especially for people with low earnings or large debt. At first, progress could appear sluggish, but each donation increases financial stability. Continued dedication is encouraged by seeing each deposit as a step toward greater freedom. People get more confident as their balance improves over time because they realize they are better equipped to handle unforeseen circumstances.

During financial crises, emergency funds also lessen reliance on debt. When an emergency arises, many people turn to credit cards or loans since they don't have any funds. Interest charges frequently result in additional financial strain that persists long after the initial need has gone, even though borrowing may offer instant comfort. Debt repayment might raise monthly costs and postpone other crucial financial objectives. A well-funded emergency fund gives people more flexibility for future planning by enabling them to handle unforeseen expenses without adding to their financial worries.

Additionally, building an emergency fund promotes mental health. One of the main causes of stress for many people and families is financial insecurity. Anxiety brought on by worrying about how to deal with unforeseen costs can have an impact on relationships, decision-making, and general quality of life. During uncertain times, it is comforting to know that emergency services are available. Instead of expecting that issues won't arise, this sense of security enables people to face obstacles with more confidence since they know they have prepared for the unexpected.

Making better decisions is another important advantage of emergency savings. When catastrophes occur, those without financial reserves could feel under pressure to make snap judgments. Due to a lack of funds, they could take out bad loans, sell important assets too soon, or put off essential repairs. By giving you time to thoroughly consider your options, an emergency fund fosters flexibility. People can make deliberate choices that support both short-term demands and long-term financial security rather than responding from a position of financial desperation.

Growth in emergency funds also promotes sound financial practices in other domains. It takes persistent discipline, careful spending, and regular planning to build savings. Overall, better money management is facilitated by these similar practices. People frequently become more conscious of wasteful spending and more dedicated to long-term financial objectives as they grow accustomed to saving on a regular basis. The discipline needed to build up an emergency fund often reinforces other sound financial practices, including debt reduction, investment growth, and budgeting.

Another significant benefit of emergency savings is flexibility. Opportunities brought about by life changes frequently necessitate short-term financial adjustments. There may be times when income is lower, or costs are higher due to relocation, family obligations, career changes, or educational possibilities. During these changes, an emergency fund gives people financial breathing room so they may make decisions based on long-term advantages rather than short-term financial strain. This adaptability lowers the dangers connected with significant life changes while promoting personal development.

Long-term investments are also safeguarded by building an emergency fund. When unforeseen costs arise, people without emergency funds occasionally take money out of retirement accounts or sell equities too soon. These acts could hinder long-term wealth accumulation and slow future financial expansion. While emergency funds take care of immediate financial requirements, investments can stay focused on their intended goal by keeping a separate emergency reserve. Both current financial stability and future financial success are supported by this division.

Adapting emergency funds as life circumstances change is another crucial factor. As a person gets married, has children, owns a home, changes careers, or expands their business, their financial obligations frequently grow over time. To offer adequate security, emergency reserves should increase in tandem with monthly expenses. Determining whether the current reserve can continue to satisfy current needs is made easier by routinely assessing financial responsibilities. This continuous assessment guarantees that emergency savings are applicable and efficient at various phases of life.

Maintaining long-term financial security requires avoiding pointless withdrawals. Every use of emergency funds should be thoroughly assessed to make sure it actually counts as an unforeseen and essential expense. Rebuilding the reserve must take precedence when funds are utilized. In addition to strengthening the practice of financial prudence, quickly replenishing emergency funds helps people prepare for future difficulties. Respecting the emergency fund contributes to maintaining its efficacy as a dependable source of financial security.

Talking about the goal of emergency savings as a family is also very beneficial. In addition to ensuring that everyone understands the significance of protecting these resources, shared understanding promotes responsible decision-making. Cooperation is strengthened, and misconceptions about when to use emergency funds are decreased when financial priorities are communicated openly—the household as a whole benefits from increased financial stability as a result of this shared commitment.

The confidence it fosters is arguably one of the biggest benefits of building an emergency fund. Knowing that unforeseen difficulties may be handled without an imminent financial crisis is the foundation of financial confidence rather than income or accumulated riches alone. Because they know they have made responsible preparations for life's uncertainties, people who have emergency funds frequently feel more at ease. This self-assurance promotes careful preparation, lessens anxiety about unforeseen costs, and supports better financial choices in many facets of life.

Growing an emergency fund ultimately entails much more than just opening a savings account. It shows a dedication to long-term planning, personal fortitude, and financial discipline. Each contribution enhances the capacity to manage uncertainty while shielding future objectives from unforeseen obstacles. People progressively build a financial safety net that offers both practical assistance and emotional comfort through regular saving, thoughtful planning, restrained spending, and frequent assessment. Over time, this expanding reserve turns into a representation of readiness, stability, and assurance, showing that long-term financial security is created not only by earning and investing but also by prudently preparing for the uncertainties that everyone may eventually encounter. People build a better foundation for long-term prosperity, more independence, and the peace of mind that comes from knowing they are prepared for whatever obstacles the future may bring by incorporating emergency savings into their daily financial routines.

Future Savings Plans

One of the most crucial financial habits a person can form is saving for the future since it offers opportunities, protection, and flexibility that would otherwise be hard to come by. Saving is more than just putting money aside once every expense has been covered. It is a conscious commitment to planning for future requirements, objectives, and unforeseen circumstances. Consistent savers are more likely to seize opportunities that enhance their quality of life and are better able to handle financial difficulties without substantially depending on debt. Over time, a well-thought-out savings plan turns modest, regular efforts into significant financial advancement by offering direction and purpose.

A common misconception is that saving is only feasible if one reaches a particular income level. Because people continue to wait for the ideal financial circumstance before starting, this mindset frequently impedes financial advancement. In actuality, regularity is more important for successful saving than the amount of each donation. Regular savings of even small amounts establish beneficial financial habits and show that advancement is achievable regardless of present income. These ingrained practices make it simpler to boost savings without making significant lifestyle adjustments as wages rise over time. One of the biggest benefits of developing financial security is starting early.

A future savings plan starts with well-defined objectives. Saving frequently feels challenging in the absence of clear goals since there is no obvious motivation for the endeavor. By tying current choices to future benefits, meaningful goals inspire people. Some people may save to create an emergency fund, buy a house, pay for college, launch a business, go on vacation, or be ready for retirement. Others might place a higher priority on helping family members, achieving financial independence, or leaving a lasting legacy for coming generations. Every savings objective is a reflection of one's own values and aspirations, which gives the process greater significance and makes it simpler to maintain during times of financial temptation.

Many people believe that the cornerstone of any future savings plan is an emergency fund. Medical emergencies, auto repairs, home upkeep, brief unemployment, and family obligations are examples of unforeseen costs that might happen at any time. People who don't have emergency reserves often turn to credit cards or loans in these circumstances, which puts more strain on their finances by adding to their debt and interest expenses. Establishing a special emergency fund gives you peace of mind and enables you to handle unforeseen circumstances without interfering with long-term financial objectives. During uncertain times, having cash reserves lowers anxiety and boosts confidence.

Just as crucial as being ready for emergencies is saving for future chances. Financial resources at the appropriate time are necessary for many worthwhile ventures. Career growth through further education, company investments, moving for better work, buying a house, or professional development are some examples of these options. Because they have planned ahead rather than responding after the event, those with established funds are better positioned to take advantage of these chances. By increasing options and lowering reliance on present income, future savings foster freedom.

The most important component of any successful savings strategy is consistency. While occasional large payments are beneficial, consistent monthly contributions frequently yield better long-term outcomes. Regardless of transient economic situations, consistency fosters discipline and permits savings to increase continuously. Because saving becomes a regular financial habit rather than a monthly decision requiring ongoing motivation, people who save regularly through scheduled transfers or payroll deductions frequently find it simpler to stick to their objectives.

Another crucial component of future savings is patience. Seldom does meaningful financial progress happen quickly, particularly when objectives call for years of planning. Some people lose hope because they only think about how far they still have to go instead of appreciating the advancements they have already made. No matter how big or small, every deposit strengthens the financial base. These little payments add up over time to form substantial resources that can support important life objectives. Recognizing the importance of patience motivates people to stick with it even when the outcomes seem minor at first.

Additionally, a future savings plan should be adaptable enough to change as circumstances do. Throughout life, income, family obligations, professional prospects, and financial priorities all inevitably change. Regularly reviewing savings objectives enables people to make deliberate changes while preserving overall progress. Contributions to savings may be raised during times of higher income in order to hasten future growth. Temporary changes may be required during difficult financial circumstances, but the practice of persistent saving should be maintained whenever possible. Plans for savings must be flexible in order to be realistic and sustainable at various phases of life.

Making the distinction between short-term and long-term savings contributes to better financial management. Goals anticipated over the next few years, such as trips, house renovations, schooling costs, or significant purchases, are usually supported by short-term savings. Retirement, financial independence, investment opportunities, and future family requirements are common goals of long-term savings. Separating these goals helps people deploy resources in accordance with various deadlines while also reducing confusion. Additionally, this strategy keeps long-term savings from being utilized for immediate needs that may otherwise be budgeted for separately.

Future financial success is significantly impacted by lifestyle decisions. The amount available for future financial objectives is impacted by every expenditure choice. This does not entail giving up all pleasurable activities or leading a life that is always constrained. Rather, it entails making deliberate decisions that strike a balance between happiness in the moment and security in the future. People who are aware of the long-term effects of their daily expenditures tend to be more frugal with their purchases and focus more of their resources on long-term objectives rather than short-term gratification.

When extra income is handled carefully, it can support future savings efforts. Opportunities to accelerate financial success include promotions, job advancement, business expansion, freelance work, and investment income. Higher income by itself, however, does not ensure greater savings if consumption rises at the same rate. It is easier to make sure that financial development results in long-term benefits rather than short-term lifestyle expansion when a percentage of every salary gain is allocated directly toward savings. This practice enables steady wealth growth while preserving financial equilibrium.

Maintaining financial discipline is crucial for preventing needless withdrawals from future savings. Many people start saving money well but subsequently spend it on things unrelated to their initial objectives. Setting up boundaries for savings accounts strengthens commitment to long-term goals while preserving financial progress. People should consider whether the expense actually supports their priorities or fulfills a fleeting desire before making a withdrawal. This methodical strategy preserves future prospects while strengthening financial decision-making.

Future savings initiatives might also be strengthened by family involvement. Open communication about common objectives increases the likelihood that a couple will support one another by making consistent financial decisions. Future generations can learn important lessons from parents who instill in their children the value of preserving. When saving is seen as a collective duty rather than an individual commitment, it takes on greater significance. Collaborating strengthens the household's feeling of purpose and promotes accountability.

Convenient tools provided by technology encourage wise saving practices. Monitoring progress is made easier by digital banking apps, goal tracking systems, automatic transfers, and financial reminders. Although these tools make things more convenient, constant activity and personal dedication are still the real sources of success. While technology can be a useful tool, people's daily habits and choices determine long-term financial progress.

Future savings strategies are kept in line with evolving objectives by routinely reviewing progress. Evaluations conducted on a monthly or quarterly basis enable people to recognize successes, pinpoint challenges, and modify contributions as needed. These evaluations support ongoing development while highlighting the link between sound financial practices and long-term success. Even if progress is slow, acknowledging it boosts self-esteem and encourages persistent saving.

Emotional well-being is also influenced by future savings. Stress is frequently brought on by financial uncertainty because people worry about unforeseen costs or upcoming obligations. Dedicated savings ease these worries by giving one a sense of control and readiness. Instead of continuously worrying about financial emergencies, this peace of mind enables people to concentrate more fully on their families, careers, health, and personal development. Consistent saving builds confidence that affects many other facets of daily life in addition to money.

In the end, setting up a savings plan for the future is an investment in both personal freedom and financial stability. Every dollar saved signifies a choice to be responsible today while planning for the future. Regular saving enhances long-term financial stability, fosters chances for meaningful growth, and increases resilience in the face of unforeseen obstacles. People can regard saving as a strong statement of dedication to the future they want to build rather than as a sacrifice. Future savings form the cornerstone of long-term financial stability and prosperity via perseverance, self-control, adaptability, and careful planning.

Saving Automatically

One of the best ways to create long-term financial security is to save automatically since it eliminates a lot of the uncertainty and inconsistency that sometimes keep people from achieving their financial objectives. When it comes to saving money, many people have excellent intentions, but good intentions by themselves do not usually result in continuous action. Savings can quickly fall to the bottom of the priority list due to everyday obligations, unforeseen costs, and the temptation to spend. By automating the saving process, people establish a dependable system that reliably allocates funds to future objectives before they may be used for other purposes. This strategy turns saving into a consistent financial habit that promotes long-term success rather than a decision that must be made on a regular basis.

The fact that automatic saving lessens the impact of emotions on financial decisions is one of its biggest advantages. Temporary emotions like enthusiasm, worry, boredom, or the need for instant gratification influence many spending decisions. Long-term plans may be hampered by these feelings when saving solely relies on personal motivation. By putting money into savings before emotional spending has a chance to happen, automatic saving eliminates a large portion of this struggle. Rather than making a monthly decision about whether or not to save, the system constantly completes the duty, freeing people to concentrate on responsibly managing the remaining income.

Additionally, automatic saving promotes the crucial idea of paying oneself first. In the hopes of having some money left over at the end of the month, many people save only after all costs have been covered. Unfortunately, because consumption automatically increases to use available income, this strategy frequently yields little to no savings. Paying yourself first entails viewing savings as a necessary financial obligation as opposed to a choice. People show that their future financial security should be given the same priority as any other monthly commitment by putting money aside as soon as they receive their salary. Over time, this straightforward change in priorities strengthens financial discipline and yields significant outcomes.

One of the most important advantages of automated saving is consistency. Rarely does building financial security depend on sporadic significant deposits. Rather, it is typically the outcome of modest, consistent efforts across several months and years. Even during hectic times when financial planning might not receive as much attention, automatic mechanisms guarantee that saving continues. Regardless of whether the contribution is made once a month, every payday, or every week, regularity enables savings to increase gradually. This consistent practice lowers the risk of forgetting or delaying donations while strengthening financial habits.

Simplifying money management is another benefit of automatic savings. It takes time, focus, and self-control to make frequent decisions about when and how much to save. By creating a preset procedure that runs without regular oversight, automation lessens this mental strain. After the system is set up, people may concentrate on other financial matters while knowing that their savings objectives are being met in the background. Because it eliminates needless barriers that could otherwise disrupt sound financial practices, simplicity frequently boosts long-term success.

Additionally, automatic saving aids people in adjusting to living within their means. The remaining funds become the monthly practical spending cap when savings are transferred as soon as income is received. People inevitably modify their spending patterns over time to conform to available funds. This change lessens the incentive to spend money that was initially meant for future objectives and promotes careful budgeting. Living comfortably within one's means promotes more long-term stability and increases financial discipline.

Automatic saving makes creating an emergency fund much simpler. If there is no reserve, unforeseen circumstances like medical bills, auto repairs, house maintenance, or a brief job loss can pose serious financial difficulties. Without constant supervision, automatic payments into a special emergency savings account progressively create a safety net. Every donation lowers dependency on borrowing during emergencies and strengthens protection against unanticipated events. People feel more confident and at ease as their emergency fund builds because they know they are getting better equipped to handle life's unforeseen events.

Long-term investing objectives are also supported by automatic saving. It takes perseverance and persistent work to save for retirement, school, home ownership, or future business prospects. Regardless of transient distractions, people can benefit from consistent growth by making regular contributions to savings or investment accounts. This methodical strategy prevents the temptation to put off payments until a more convenient moment while allowing financial growth to happen gradually. Consistent deposits frequently emerge over time as one of the key elements influencing significant financial growth.

The fact that automated saving lessens financial stress is another significant advantage. Concerns about whether they are saving enough for the future induce anxiety in a lot of people. By guaranteeing that progress continues on a regular basis, automatic systems offer assurance. Knowing that savings are steadily increasing, even with small amounts, gives one a sense of stability and success. This assurance lessens concern about future readiness while motivating people to stick to their long-term financial strategies.

By fostering a long-term outlook, automatic saving also encourages patience. Rarely do abrupt shifts or exceptional occurrences lead to financial success. Rather, it grows gradually as a result of consistent good deeds. The knowledge that long-term prosperity is the product of persistence rather than speed is reinforced when savings grow month after month. Because they understand that each contribution is a step closer to financial independence, this viewpoint encourages people to stay dedicated even when things seem to be moving slowly.

Another useful aspect of automated saving is flexibility. Throughout life, one's financial situation may vary as a result of unanticipated bills, family obligations, career growth, or economic situations. In most cases, automatic contributions can be modified to reflect changing conditions. Contributions to savings may be raised to speed up progress during times of higher income. Contributions may be lowered while keeping up the saving habit during brief financial challenges. This flexibility enables people to maintain long-term discipline without incurring needless financial hardship.

By showcasing a person's dedication to long-term objectives, automatic saving also boosts financial confidence. The idea that disciplined habits yield significant outcomes is strengthened by each successful transfer. Because they continuously uphold their commitment to saving, people start to see themselves as competent financial managers. Additional sound financial practices like cutting back on wasteful spending, boosting investments, enhancing budgeting, and seizing new chances for both professional and personal development are frequently prompted by this increased self-assurance.

Automatic savings can also be very beneficial to families. Regular savings programs help parents prepare for future family requirements while modeling appropriate financial conduct for their kids. Cooperation and shared responsibility are promoted by automatic payments to emergency savings, school funds, family trips, or large expenditures. Family members can better appreciate the need to prepare ahead of time and make careful financial decisions by having candid conversations about savings objectives. Generational financial foundations are strengthened by these common practices.

Automatic saving also lessens the desire to spend unforeseen cash, which is a significant benefit. When there is no plan in place for their utilization, bonuses, tax refunds, pay raises, or additional profits frequently vanish rapidly. By including recurring transfers for a portion of these funds, you can make sure that at least some of the extra income goes toward long-term financial security instead of being completely used for transient expenses. By using this tactic, people can continue to improve their financial situation while also strengthening their position in the future.

It's also crucial to routinely review automated savings arrangements. Contributions should be assessed to make sure they stay in line with current priorities as financial objectives change. People might decide to boost their savings rates, open more accounts for certain goals, or reroute contributions to new opportunities. Frequent assessment encourages ongoing progress toward shifting financial goals while maintaining the savings strategy's relevance.

One of the most important things to learn from automatic saving is that processes are more important for financial success than just motivation. Naturally, motivation fluctuates based on situations, feelings, and everyday obligations. However, despite brief shifts in excitement, systems continue to function. People eliminate a lot of the uncertainty that frequently impedes steady progress by establishing dependable financial practices. Automatic saving shows that developing dependable habits that continuously support future objectives is just as important to building long-term wealth as increasing income.

In the end, automated saving is a useful and effective habit that turns financial planning into regular action. It boosts long-term commitment, lowers emotional spending, promotes discipline without requiring constant effort, and gradually increases financial security through consistent payments. These automatic payments build up over time into valuable assets that support investments, personal objectives, emergencies, and increased financial freedom. People build a solid basis for long-term prosperity by eliminating needless obstacles and integrating saving into daily living. Automatic saving becomes a crucial habit that helps people make better daily decisions and gets them ready for a future with more stability, confidence, opportunity, and peace of mind via perseverance, consistency, careful preparation, and dependable financial systems.

Preparing For Tomorrow

One of the most important skills anybody can cultivate is the capacity to plan financially for the future, since decisions taken today have an impact on tomorrow. Every financial decision either creates future constraints or improves future chances. Many people think that saving money is only about accumulating more cash, but there is much more to it than that. It lessens the stress that results from life without preparation, gives freedom to explore worthwhile opportunities, and offers security during unpredictable times. This chapter is important because it promotes a change from responding to financial situations to confidently and intentionally anticipating them. The desire to face the future with stability and peace of mind, rather than fear of it, is what motivates preparation. Every contribution lays the groundwork for future success when saving becomes a deliberate habit rather than an infrequent action.

By putting the ideas discussed in this chapter into practice, people's perspectives on time and money are altered. Savings are no longer seen as money that cannot be spent, but rather as a resource that opens up opportunities for the future. Every sum laid away signifies a choice to put long-term stability ahead of immediate satisfaction. People gain confidence because they are aware that they are progressively getting ready for unforeseen costs, significant life events, career changes, and personal objectives. Since preparedness has already started, financial emergencies lose much of their emotional impact. When resources are purposefully allocated to long-term goals, they become more achievable. This methodical approach turns financial management from a sequence of actions into a deliberate, purpose-driven process. The biggest shift frequently happens on the inside, as discipline takes the place of reluctance and confidence takes the place of uncertainty.

Ignoring these guidelines can have far-reaching effects that go well beyond monetary hardship. Even minor unforeseen costs can cause a great deal of worry if saving is not a regular practice. When there is no safety net, medical expenses, auto repairs, home upkeep, short-term unemployment, or family problems can quickly result in debt. The lack of means to support education, career growth, relocation, or investment may also cause opportunities to be lost. Living unprepared frequently starts a vicious cycle where each unforeseen circumstance results in yet another financial hardship. Because short-term survival always takes precedence over long-term planning, this pattern eventually erodes confidence and restricts options. The work needed to accumulate funds over time steadily is sometimes far less expensive than the lack of preparation.

Purposeful saving has an impact on many facets of real life. Because crucial decisions are no longer dominated by financial uncertainty, families enjoy more emotional stability. People are given the freedom to choose their careers based on long-term objectives rather than short-term financial constraints. Parents get better equipped to help their kids through significant life changes. Because consistent habits have already been formed, retirement planning becomes less daunting. When planning lowers stress, financial disputes become less frequent, which frequently improves personal relationships. Above all, saving with purpose leads to freedom. It enables people to make choices based on opportunity and values rather than necessity and fear.

By the end of this chapter, you will be able to create a practical financial reserve that boosts confidence while offering more flexibility for future opportunities and challenges, set meaningful savings goals that support both anticipated and unexpected future needs, and develop consistent saving habits that fit your income and lifestyle without sacrificing long-term progress.

Take Jonathan as an example, who thought that if his income grew, he could start saving. He put off the habit for years because there was always another expense that needed to be attended to right away. His car eventually needed extensive repairs, so he had to rely on high-interest borrowing to keep working. His viewpoint was altered by that encounter. He made a commitment to set aside a tiny sum from each pay check, no matter how small, rather than waiting for perfect conditions. Instead of viewing his savings as optional extra cash, he saw them as a monthly obligation. His emergency fund steadily grew as the months went by. Two years later, another unforeseen repair came up, but he paid for it without taking out a loan or upsetting his financial plans. Jonathan came to see that the discipline of starting was more significant than the amount he had initially saved.

Uncertainty had given way to preparation, which increased his confidence.

This idea is effectively illustrated with a short narrative. The approach of the rainy season was anticipated by two farmers. Before fixing his irrigation system and stockpiling supplies, the first farmer waited for ominous clouds to form. By then, the task was challenging, costly, and unpleasant due to the constant rain. While the weather was quiet, the second farmer made preparations months in advance. He built fences, stored seeds, fixed equipment, and made sure everything was prepared before the storms hit. Both farmers faced the same weather when the rains finally arrived, but only one felt confident rather than terrified. The same concept applies to financial preparation. Although obstacles are unavoidable, careful planning determines whether they turn into short-term annoyances or long-term setbacks.

Building a lighthouse before the storm arrives is a helpful metaphor for intentional conserving. In hazardous weather, when ships are already battling strong waves, a lighthouse is not built. It is meticulously constructed over time during calm conditions so that it can offer advice in the event of storms. In personal finance, savings serve the same purpose. Each donation fortifies a reliable source of stability that becomes indispensable in times of uncertainty. Although it doesn't stop storms, the lighthouse makes it easier for people to traverse them safely. Similarly, intentional saving offers the stability required to confront life's unforeseen catastrophes with more resilience and confidence, but it cannot completely prevent them.

Use the Save Secure Succeed Framework to start putting these concepts into practice right away. Start by deciding which financial scenarios, such as crises, future prospects, school, retirement, travel, or significant purchases, you wish to plan for. Next, set a reasonable savings goal for each goal without being deterred by the total amount needed. Break each goal up into manageable weekly or monthly contributions. Then, as soon as revenue is received, set up regular payments to automate the saving process whenever possible. Consider these contributions as obligations rather than choices. At the conclusion of each month, evaluate your progress, acknowledge consistent success, and modify your donation amount if your circumstances or income change. Repeat this procedure until saving is no longer a constant source of motivation but rather an automatic part of your financial routine.

This framework's practicality is what makes it effective. Many people put off saving because they think big sums of money are necessary to make significant progress. In actuality, consistent efforts typically yield better outcomes than sporadic significant contributions. Regular small deposits profit from time and discipline. Additionally, they reinforce the practice of planning before situations call for quick action. Every donation, no matter how big or small, is another choice to put future security ahead of convenience.

Realizing that saving is not an act of deprivation is another crucial lesson. It is a deliberate act of choice. Today's money is not being lost. It is being given a worthwhile purpose that fulfills needs and goals for the future. The emotional experience of saving is altered by this viewpoint. Instead of feeling constrained, people start to realize that each contribution expands their freedom in the future. Because they are already financially prepared, they are better equipped to handle crises with composure, seize desirable chances, and make critical life decisions with more assurance.

Additionally, saving with a purpose fosters patience, which is crucial for long-term financial success. While instant satisfaction is frequently emphasized in modern culture, significant financial advancement typically happens gradually. Discipline is necessary to wait for savings to increase, but it also fortifies many other financial practices, such as prudent spending, cautious planning, and smart investing. Small everyday choices made with patience can add up to amazing long-term outcomes that would have appeared unattainable at the start of the trip.

Recognizing that financial planning should change as one moves through different phases of life is equally crucial. The primary goals of early savings could be short-term stability and emergencies. Education, home ownership, business prospects, retirement, and ensuring future generations have financial security are examples of later objectives. The fundamental habit doesn't alter, even if the specific goals do. People who regularly plan for the future are better able to adjust to new chances and responsibilities in life comfortably.

Consider whether your present financial practices are setting you up for future success or making you more susceptible to unforeseen difficulties. Which significant objective merits special savings starting today? Which wasteful spending could be cut to improve your security in the future without lowering your standard of living? If you knew you were ready for an unforeseen financial disaster, how would it affect your confidence? What modest saving practice could you start right now that would help your finances for many years to come? What effects will the decisions you make this week have on the chances you have tomorrow?

One deliberate choice to get ready before it becomes essential is the first step towards any secure financial future. The resources you depend on tomorrow are the habits you form today. Continue constructing your future with perseverance, consistency, and purpose, knowing that each effort will improve your capacity to handle both anticipated possibilities and unforeseen obstacles. One deliberate choice at a time builds long-term financial confidence. Each act of preparation becomes an investment in a future characterized by stability, freedom, resilience, and the enduring peace of mind that comes from knowing you are prepared for whatever tomorrow may bring as you continue to move forward with discipline and resolve.

CHAPTER VI

Debt Reduction Strategies

Understanding Debt Costs

Since borrowing money always has repercussions that go beyond the initial amount borrowed, understanding debt costs is crucial to attaining long-term financial security. When handled sensibly and put to good use, debt can be a helpful financial instrument, but when people don't realize how much it really costs, it can also become a major barrier. Instead of thinking about the overall amount they will eventually return, many people think about whether they can afford the monthly payment. This narrow viewpoint frequently results in financial choices that cause needless stress for many years. Gaining a better grasp of debt costs enables people to manage their current responsibilities, borrow money more sensibly, and safeguard future financial prospects.

Debt is a commitment to spend money now and promise to pay it back later, usually with extra expenses called interest. Interest is the cost of borrowing money and reimburses lenders for taking on the financial risk. When considered as a monthly payment, interest may seem small, but over a number of years, its cumulative effect can significantly raise the overall cost of a transaction. Even a loan that sounds reasonable at first could end up costing far more to repay. Understanding this distinction motivates people to consider borrowing options more thoroughly before taking on debt.

Focusing only on monthly affordability is one of the most frequent mistakes people make. Because it easily fits into a budget, a reduced monthly payment frequently seems appealing. However, the total amount of interest paid typically rises when repayment is spread out over a longer time frame. Smaller monthly payments offer flexibility in the short term, but they frequently result in much higher overall costs. Knowing this link enables people to see that the cheapest monthly payment isn't always the best long-term financial option.

Credit cards are an obvious illustration of how debt expenses may mount up quickly when balances are not paid. Because they don't need as much cash right away, many credit card users merely pay the minimum amount each month. Although this method avoids late payments, it frequently permits interest to accrue over long stretches of time. The initial purchase gets more costly as interest compounds, potentially costing several times its original amount. Whenever feasible, paying more than the minimum amount shortens the payback period, improves long-term financial health, and lowers overall interest.

The financial impact of various types of debt varies. Mortgages, student loans, business loans, auto loans, and personal loans all have distinct uses and entail different financial risks, interest rates, and payback schedules. While certain forms of borrowing are mainly used to finance consumption, others promote long-term asset creation or income growth. Knowing these differences enables people to assess whether borrowing improves their financial situation in the long run or offers short-term satisfaction at a higher cost.

The real cost of debt goes beyond just interest. The financial burden may be further increased by loan fees, service charges, insurance requirements, late payment penalties, and other related costs. When evaluating financing options, people who consider advertising interest rates might miss these extra expenses. Examining all loan terms thoroughly before committing promotes better financial decision-making and helps avoid unforeseen costs.

Additionally, debt results in potential costs that are frequently disregarded. Each interest payment is a sum of money that could be used for investments, savings, education, company ventures, or other worthwhile financial objectives. Repaying loans is an essential commitment, but having too much debt restricts one's ability to generate wealth in the future. Understanding these opportunity costs urges people to take out loans only in situations when the long-term advantages clearly exceed the associated financial costs.

Financial debt frequently has emotional repercussions as well. Stress, anxiety, uncertainty, and diminished confidence are often brought on by large debt levels. Because monthly payments take up a large amount of their income, people with enormous financial responsibilities may feel constrained when making decisions about their careers, moving, launching enterprises, or pursuing personal chances. Relationships, physical health, productivity, and general quality of life can all be impacted by this emotional strain. Therefore, lowering needless debt promotes both improved personal well-being and stronger finances.

Before taking on new financial commitments, responsible borrowing starts with a thorough assessment. It is possible to ascertain whether borrowing is actually required by posing intelligent inquiries. People should think about whether the purchase advances a worthwhile long-term goal, whether there are less costly options, whether savings could achieve the same aim, and whether payback is still reasonable in light of shifting financial conditions. Impulsive financial decisions that have long-term effects are frequently avoided by delaying borrowing long enough to consider these issues.

By providing funds for both anticipated and unforeseen costs, conserving money lessens reliance on debt. Without using high-interest loans, emergency reserves enable people to handle short-term financial challenges. Similarly, saving for future purchases allows people to pay with their own funds instead of taking out loans to cover expenses. Every dollar saved up front has the potential to increase financial independence and minimize future interest expenses.

Knowing the price of debt also promotes more deliberate spending. Long before the loan is paid off in full, many purchases that are financed by borrowing lose value. Purchases of consumer goods, technology, clothing, and entertainment can result in short-term pleasure but long-term financial commitments. Acknowledging this disparity allows people to choose between purchases that provide value over time and those that merely fulfill immediate needs. Thorough assessment aids in matching borrowing choices with significant personal priorities.

In order to lower overall borrowing costs, debt repayment solutions are crucial. Whenever feasible, paying more than the minimum amount due reduces principal amounts faster, which lowers overall interest costs. Consistent additional payments over time frequently result in far shorter payback terms and better cash flow for long-term financial objectives. When used consistently throughout the course of a loan, even small additional payments might result in significant savings.

Increasing one's financial literacy improves one's capacity for responsible debt management. People can assess financial products more confidently if they are aware of interest computations, loan conditions, credit ratings, repayment plans, and borrowing options. While promoting well-informed decision-making based on precise understanding, education lessens reliance on presumptions. People are better able to identify both advantageous borrowing opportunities and needless financial dangers as their financial literacy increases.

Responsible debt management is further supported by keeping a realistic budget. Knowing precisely how much money is left over after necessities enables people to assess whether taking on more debt is financially feasible. Budgets also highlight ways to cut back on wasteful expenditure, freeing up funds for savings or debt reduction. Financial planning guarantees that borrowing choices promote long-term stability instead of continuing to put a strain on finances.

Another important trait in lowering debt payments is patience. Because finance and financing are readily available, modern society frequently promotes instant pleasure. However, borrowing expenses are often completely eliminated when purchases are postponed until adequate savings have accumulated. While waiting may necessitate self-control, it also lowers long-term costs and increases financial independence. Those who cultivate patience frequently find more fulfillment in accomplishing objectives through careful planning as opposed to depending on quick borrowing.

Maintaining awareness of financial progress is facilitated by routinely monitoring debt obligations. Keeping an eye on loan balances, payback schedules, and interest expenses inspires people while pointing out areas for development. When they see quantifiable progress toward financial freedom, those who monitor their lowering debt amounts frequently feel more confident. When income rises or financial conditions improve, these frequent assessments also stimulate adjustments, enabling quicker repayment whenever feasible.

In the end, knowing the consequences of debt enables people to make better financial choices that promote long-term stability and prosperity. Consideration should always be given to borrowing, taking into account both its possible advantages and its long-term obligations. Every financial commitment affects future prospects by limiting the amount of money left over for investing, saving, personal development, and fulfilling life experiences. People develop better connections with debt while safeguarding their long-term financial future by comprehending interest, assessing overall repayment costs, avoiding needless borrowing, upholding disciplined repayment behaviors, and expanding their financial literacy. Thoughtful borrowing increases freedom, lowers needless stress, and promotes the steady building of long-term financial security over the course of a lifetime when paired with regular saving and prudent financial planning.

Payment Priority Methods

It takes more than just paying bills as they come in to manage financial commitments effectively. It entails developing a careful structure that supports long-term financial stability and guarantees that available revenue is allocated first to the most crucial obligations. Payment priority approaches offer a methodical way to determine which bills should be paid right away, which debts need more attention, and which financial objectives should be consistently funded. People who set clear payment priorities have more control over their finances, experience less needless stress, and become more confident in their financial choices rather than responding to financial strain every month. In addition to preventing missed payments, a well-planned payment plan offers chances to invest, save, and gradually enhance overall financial well-being.

Determining necessary living expenditures is the first step in developing a successful payment priority system. Housing, food, utilities, transportation, healthcare, and other everyday essentials are among them. Since these responsibilities directly impact stability, health, and personal safety, they should always be given top priority.

Serious repercussions, such as eviction, power disconnection, transportation issues, or restricted access to medical treatment, can swiftly result from failing to make payments on necessary bills. Every other financial decision may be made on a solid basis created by safeguarding these necessities.

Once basic living expenses have been covered, focus should turn to making minimal debt payments. Minimum monthly payments that must be made on time are frequently required for credit cards, personal loans, student loans, mortgages, and auto loans. By fulfilling these commitments on a regular basis, credit history is safeguarded, expensive late fees are avoided, and balances are kept from increasing due to further penalties. Maintaining minimal payments shows financial discipline and keeps accounts in good standing while a more comprehensive repayment plan is devised, even though it can take some time to pay off debt.

Extra money that is available can be used for accelerated debt payback after minimum debt obligations have been met. Many people who are financially prosperous decide to keep minimal payments on all other accounts while concentrating additional payments on one debt at a time. Because concentrated payments decrease balances more quickly than dispersing excess funds across several responsibilities, this targeted technique eliminates debt more effectively. Every loan that is paid off in full releases more cash flow, accelerating the process of achieving total financial freedom. Seeing debts vanish has psychological benefits that promote ongoing self-control and strengthen sound financial practices.

When money is left over at the end of the month, saving should never be considered an afterthought. Rather, savings should have a specific position in terms of payment priorities. By setting up an emergency fund, people can avoid using debt in the event of unforeseen costs. Even well-planned budgets can be disrupted by medical emergencies, auto repairs, home maintenance, or unexpected income loss. These circumstances can be handled without escalating financial strain or accruing new debt thanks to devoted savings. Long-term financial security is strengthened by regular, albeit modest, contributions to emergency reserves.

Payment priorities should also carefully take retirement funds into account. Delaying payments frequently results in missed opportunities for long-term gain through compound profits, even though retirement may seem far off. Later in life, even little donations made regularly over a long period of time might result in substantial financial resources. A balanced financial mentality that values both current commitments and future independence is demonstrated by prioritizing retirement alongside current obligations. Increasing retirement savings increases flexibility for future life decisions and eventually lowers the chance of financial difficulties in later years.

Priority payment plans also promote careful preparation for anticipated future costs. Financial surprises shouldn't arise from yearly insurance premiums, property taxes, educational costs, holiday celebrations, and scheduled vacations. Budget difficulties and last-minute borrowing are avoided by setting aside modest monthly sums for these anticipated expenses. By converting high one-time costs into reasonable monthly obligations, this approach eases financial strain and promotes year-round budgeting.

Differentiating between necessities and wants is a crucial component of payment prioritizing. When discretionary spending often conflicts with necessary commitments, numerous financial difficulties result. While eating out, entertainment, luxury goods, and impulsive shopping may offer momentary satisfaction, these costs should never get in the way of essential payments, debt repayment, or savings objectives. Delaying pointless purchases improves self-control and guarantees that financial resources stay in line with long-term goals rather than transient wants.

The efficiency of payment priorities can be greatly increased by automation. Setting up automated payments for savings contributions, debt obligations, and necessary expenses lowers the possibility of forgetting due dates while fostering consistency in money management. Much of the emotional decision-making that frequently goes along with money management is eliminated by automated solutions. People create dependable habits that continue to function even during hectic or difficult times, rather than depending on memory or inspiration each month. This regularity reduces costly errors and fosters better financial habits.

Since financial situations naturally change over time, regular review and adjustment are still crucial. It's possible for income to rise, expenses to change, debts to be paid off, or new financial objectives to arise. A payment priority system should be adaptable enough to meet both short-term demands and long-term goals. People can discover areas for improvement, reallocate available resources, and sustain steady progress toward financial independence by reviewing their financial priorities every few months. Ongoing assessment guarantees that financial choices are deliberate rather than reflexive reactions to shifting conditions.

Priorities for payments should also take into account one's ideals and aspirations in life. After fulfilling their basic financial commitments, some people may decide to put education, home ownership, company development, charitable giving, or family support first. Money becomes a tool for attaining desired outcomes rather than just covering expenses when payment selections are in line with significant personal aspirations. This leads to increased satisfaction. Long-term commitment is encouraged by purpose-driven financial management, which also lessens the desire to spend money needlessly.

Payment priorities may need to be temporarily adjusted due to unforeseen financial difficulties. People may be forced to concentrate solely on basic living expenses until stability returns due to job loss, illness, decreased income, or emergency spending. Keeping lines of communication open with lenders, reducing frivolous spending, and safeguarding necessities become particularly crucial during these times. When faced with financial difficulties, being adaptable helps people recover more successfully while reducing long-term financial harm.

In the end, more stability, confidence, and financial resilience result from the development of consistent payment priority systems. People acquire a clear sense of where each dollar should go and why each payment matters, rather than feeling overburdened by multiple responsibilities. This methodical approach lowers uncertainty, promotes prudent financial decision-making, and fosters consistent advancement toward significant financial objectives. Disciplined payment priorities eventually turn into automatic routines that improve financial stability, lessen reliance on debt, and provide long-term chances for wealth accumulation through careful daily financial choices.

Avoiding Future Debt

One of the most beneficial financial habits one can cultivate is avoiding future debt since it increases prospects for long-term wealth, protects income, and maintains financial flexibility. While some types of borrowing could be required in specific situations, using debt as a regular way to cover daily costs frequently results in financial strain that gets harder to manage. Every financial commitment made today affects decisions made in the future by lowering the amount of money available for investing, saving, and accomplishing worthwhile objectives. People can experience more financial freedom and build a more secure future for themselves and their families by developing behaviors that lessen the need for borrowing.

Developing a mindset that prioritizes preparedness over reaction is one of the best strategies to prevent future debt. Because they are unprepared for anticipated or unforeseen needs, many people take out loans. When adequate resources are not accessible, borrowing is frequently required for things like auto repairs, medical expenditures, home maintenance, educational costs, or temporary income reductions. Instead of depending on credit cards or loans, people can respond confidently when they are prepared for these circumstances through regular preparation. While financial planning cannot completely eliminate life's obstacles, it significantly lowers the possibility that those obstacles will lead to long-term debt.

One of the best ways to prevent future borrowing is to establish and keep an emergency fund. Unexpected expenses are a common occurrence rather than an anomaly. Family situations happen, cars need to be repaired, medical issues arise, and appliances eventually need to be replaced. These circumstances frequently force people to go for credit in order to satisfy their immediate demands since they lack financial reserves. An emergency fund offers a safety net that makes it possible to handle unforeseen expenses without interfering with long-term financial objectives or adding to repayment commitments. Reliance on borrowed funds can be considerably decreased with even modest emergency savings accumulated over time.

Another crucial rule for preventing future debt is to live below one's means. Many financial problems result from spending continuously exceeding available resources rather than from poor income. Adopting a more expensive lifestyle through larger homes, newer cars, luxury purchases, frequent eating out, or pricey entertainment is simple when income rises. While these options may give immediate satisfaction, they also increase financial burdens and restrict flexibility. Making the decision to live comfortably within one's means reduces the need for borrowing and leaves space for investing, saving, and future opportunity preparation.

By giving each dollar a distinct purpose, creating a realistic budget helps avoid debt. Spending frequently becomes reactive rather than deliberate in the absence of a budget. The amount of available income is gradually reduced by little daily purchases, impulsive expenditures, and neglected regular expenses until borrowing seems to be the only option for more significant financial demands. Before money is spent, a practical budget determines future priorities, discretionary spending, savings targets, and necessary expenses. This degree of structure guarantees that available revenue meets both current obligations and future goals while lowering financial surprises.

Avoiding needless debt also requires an understanding of the distinction between needs and wants. Housing, food, transportation, healthcare, utilities, and other essentials that support day-to-day living are examples of essential needs. Wants are not necessary for basic well-being, but they do improve comfort, convenience, or enjoyment. People frequently finance items that only temporarily satisfy their needs and create long-term repayment obligations when they confuse wants with needs. Carefully considering purchases before making them promotes more prudent financial choices and minimizes needless borrowing.

Another frequent factor contributing to future debt is impulsive expenditure. Rather than being well planned, many purchases are made in reaction to feelings. People may spend more than they can afford due to stress, enthusiasm, boredom, celebration, or social pressure. Impulsive purchases are especially simple when using credit cards and online shopping because payments are made later rather than right away. Developing routines like delaying non-essential purchases, weighing options, or talking to dependable family members about big purchases promotes more deliberate decision-making while lowering emotional spending.

Increasing savings for anticipated costs further lessens reliance on borrowing. Vacations, house renovations, schooling, holiday celebrations, and car replacements are just a few of the major purchases that can be planned well in advance. Regularly setting away funds for these future requirements enables people to make payments using savings instead of credit. Planned saving avoids interest rates and long-term repayment commitments while converting huge expenses into attainable financial goals.

Gaining more financial literacy also helps prevent debt in the future. People are better able to make responsible financial decisions if they are aware of interest rates, loan terms, repayment plans, and the actual cost of borrowing. Instead of encouraging impulsive borrowing, education promotes careful planning. Gaining knowledge about financial planning, investing, saving, insurance, and budgeting boosts confidence and lowers the risk of making expensive financial errors. Knowledge enables one to identify both advantageous financial opportunities and needless risks.

By increasing long-term earning potential, career growth helps prevent debt. Opportunities for higher income and more stable careers are increased by investing in education, professional skills, certificates, or real-world experience. Having a high earning potential makes it simpler to handle financial obligations while generating more funds for investments and saves. While income by itself does not ensure financial success, a combination of higher income and sound money management practices greatly lowers the need for borrowing over the course of a lifetime.

Keeping up sufficient insurance coverage also aids in avoiding debt in the future. If adequate coverage is lacking, medical emergencies, property damage, accidents, or unanticipated responsibility can result in significant financial problems. Even while regular premium payments are necessary for insurance, these expenses are frequently much less than the financial ramifications of suffering significant losses without coverage. With the right insurance, people may handle unforeseen risks without depleting their savings or severely depending on loans in trying times.

Effective financial communication helps families avoid debt. Couples are more likely to make consistent decisions that promote long-term stability when they are transparent about their financial objectives, spending priorities, and budgeting choices. In addition to promoting cooperation in cost management and future needs planning, shared understanding lessens misconceptions. By teaching kids the value of budgeting, saving, and avoiding needless borrowing at a young age, teaching them responsible money practices also helps them be financially secure in the future.

One of the most important personal traits for avoiding debt is patience. Through simple financing choices, payment plans, and easily accessible credit, modern culture frequently promotes instant satisfaction. However, there are a number of benefits to holding off on making significant purchases until enough money has been saved. Delaying purchases strengthens financial discipline, eliminates interest expenses, and promotes careful decision-making. People who are patient frequently find that some desired purchases become less important with time, freeing up resources for more important objectives.

Long-term debt avoidance is also supported by boosting confidence through minor financial achievements. Consistently paying bills, building savings, paying off debt, and reaching financial goals all serve to reinforce good habits and show that prudent money management yields significant outcomes. Every success increases the desire to keep making prudent financial choices rather than reverting to needless borrowing habits. Future financial stability is largely dependent on the confidence that is developed through steady progress.

Frequent financial evaluations assist in spotting possible issues before they worsen. People can identify shifting situations and make appropriate adjustments by keeping an eye on their income, expenses, savings, debt levels, and financial goals. Corrective action can be taken before borrowing becomes necessary if spending starts to rise more quickly than income or savings contributions start to fall. Ongoing financial awareness encourages proactive decision-making rather than waiting until financial challenges become overwhelming.

Refusing every chance to borrow money is not the same as avoiding future debt. There may be occasions where judicious borrowing supports meaningful long-term goals, such as acquiring a home, funding schooling, or establishing a business. The distinction is in making these choices with meticulous preparation, practical repayment plans, and a thorough comprehension of the advantages and obligations. Instead of making up for bad spending patterns or inadequate planning, borrowing should promote financial growth.

Ultimately, avoiding future debt is about developing a financial life focused on stability, discipline, and conscious choices. Financial independence is strengthened by every choice to save rather than borrow, to plan rather than react, and to put long-term security ahead of short-term gratification. Consistent budgeting, emergency savings, judicious spending, constant learning, job advancement, and frequent financial evaluations all work together to lessen dependency on debt while extending future options. These practices eventually lead to enhanced financial resilience, peace of mind, and the ability to pursue worthwhile objectives without being constrained by needless financial responsibilities. By making intelligent everyday decisions and preparing properly for the future, individuals can protect themselves from needless debt while building a strong and durable financial foundation that supports prosperity for many years to come.

Freedom Through Discipline

Realizing that discipline, not luck, is the key to achieving actual independence is one of the biggest benefits of developing better financial habits. Although discipline's true goal is to create more chances for the future, many individuals identify it with constraint, sacrifice, or the loss of enjoyment. Every deliberate financial choice made today lessens needless obligations in the future. The ideas discussed in this chapter are important because they show that hope alone does not make financial commitments go away. Consistent activity, thoughtful planning, and a readiness to make choices that promote long-term stability rather than short-term comfort are how they are overcome. Every deliberate contribution boosts financial confidence, lessens stress in the future, and opens up more space for development. When discipline becomes a daily habit rather than a sporadic endeavor, the path to financial independence begins.

The balance of financial responsibilities is not the only thing that is altered when the teachings from this chapter are applied. It changes how people view money, accountability, and making their own decisions. People who regularly follow these guidelines become more deliberate in their earning, spending, saving, and management of all available resources. They start making decisions that promote long-term security rather than fleeting happiness. As progress becomes quantifiable instead of unpredictable, financial confidence rises. With each steady stride ahead, responsibilities become easier to handle, which progressively reduces stress. Increased financial stability and better communication are beneficial to families. When more money is available to support future objectives rather than past choices, opportunities that previously appeared unattainable become feasible; this change permeates every aspect of life, substituting confidence for dissatisfaction and preparation for uncertainty.

Ignoring these ideas frequently results in a completely different future. Unmanaged financial commitments seldom stay the same. Interest keeps mounting, minimum payments take up more and more money, and it gets harder to take advantage of future chances. Because too much of their income is spent elsewhere, people may put off crucial objectives like buying a house, launching a business, going back to school, or getting ready for retirement. As financial strain impacts relationships, employment choices, and general well-being, emotional stress frequently rises. Unhealthy financial habits get harder to break the longer they persist. What starts out as a modest commitment may later restrict one's freedom, self-assurance, and ability to make personal decisions. The repercussions of not practicing financial discipline do not go away. It frequently enables them to develop silently until they become considerably more difficult to defeat.

Consistent financial discipline has a surprising impact on actual life because it goes beyond the numbers on a statement. People who gradually cut back on their financial responsibilities tend to have better emotional health since they stop worrying about money all the time. Because resources are now accessible for important goals rather than needless interest expenses, families experience better stability. Financial pressure no longer forces decisions based solely on immediate income, making career opportunities easier to pursue. Because there are fewer financial commitments vying for available resources, savings grow more organically. Consistent progress increases flexibility, making long-term investments feasible. The biggest advantage is not just having fewer responsibilities, but also having the assurance that your future is being formed more and more by deliberate choices rather than past errors.

By the end of this chapter, you will be able to identify spending and repayment patterns that enhance long-term financial stability, develop a practical plan for lowering financial obligations through consistent action, and uphold disciplined financial behaviors that promote increased self-assurance, flexibility, and long-term financial independence.

Think about Rebecca's experience, who had a number of debts that had accrued over many years. Every month seemed to conclude with little discernible progress, so at first she thought the situation was too stressful to get better. Rather than giving up, she came up with a straightforward strategy. She continued to make the necessary payments on all of her obligations while allocating any excess funds to a single priority balance. By cooking at home, delaying impulsive purchases, and selling things she no longer required, she also cut down on wasteful spending. She rerouted the previous payment toward the following priority each time an obligation was fulfilled. Even while the first year's progress seemed sluggish, it eventually picked up speed as each balance was paid off, freeing up more money each month. Rebecca became financially independent of such responsibilities after a few years. In retrospect, she saw that the biggest accomplishment was not just getting rid of financial obligations but also cultivating the self-control that altered her attitude toward money forever.

This lesson is further illustrated through a short narrative. An experienced guide was questioned by a rookie mountain climber about how anyone could reach the highest peak without being deterred by the distance. Grinning, the guide gestured to the meandering path. No one climbs a mountain in a single step, he clarified. With each cautious step, the climber gains strength and gets closer to the summit. People who look at the far-off summit all the time frequently lose motivation and give up. People who concentrate on making the next sensible move eventually get to locations they previously thought were unattainable. The same is true for financial advancement. Remarkable accomplishments that initially appear unattainable are the result of persistent action repeated over time.

Taking hefty stones out of a backpack while traveling is a helpful metaphor for financial discipline. Imagine trekking a challenging terrain with a backpack full of extra weight. Every mile takes more work, every climb becomes more taxing, and every chance to move freely feels constrained by the weight being carried. Every financial commitment is like one of those stones. The trip gets lighter, quicker, and more pleasurable with each responsible payment. One stone at a time is the process of discipline. Continuing until the backpack no longer stops you from confidently traveling toward your target leads to freedom.

Use the Focus Progress Repeat Framework to start putting these ideas into practice right away. Start by listing all of your current debts, along with the amount owed, the cost of interest, and the necessary payment. Clearly arrange this information so that each requirement is apparent rather than unclear. Next, select a priority obligation that will continue to receive minimum payments on all other obligations while receiving every additional payment that is available. Examine your monthly spending and note any costs that can be cut without materially lowering your standard of living. Allocate all available funds to the selected priority. Measure your progress at the end of each month, acknowledge any improvement, no matter how small, and keep using the same approach until the first task is finished. Transfer the past payment amount to the next priority after it has been removed, then repeat the procedure. Until all needless financial burdens have been eliminated, persistently repeat this cycle. Avoid taking on new, needless responsibilities during the process to ensure that each advancement results in long-lasting progress.

This framework's simplicity and sustainability are its strongest points. Instead of making drastic, hard-to-maintain changes, it promotes gradual advancement through doable steps. Every accomplishment boosts motivation to keep going while boosting confidence. Little successes serve as potent reminders that long-lasting change is occurring. Visible progress encourages disciplined behavior, which makes consistency easier.

Realizing that failures should never be used as justifications for giving up on advancement is another crucial lesson. Your progress may periodically be slowed by unforeseen costs, brief income decreases, or shifting family commitments. The work that has already been done is not erased by these difficulties. They need to be carefully adjusted before moving forward. Financial discipline is determined by moving forward in spite of obstacles rather than by avoiding them all. Flexibility combined with commitment creates resilience that supports lasting success.

It's also important to understand that, rather than just eliminating issues, lowering financial commitments opens up options. Every payment that is no longer needed can be used for business expansion, charitable giving, education, investing, saving, or other worthwhile endeavors. As a result, practicing financial discipline turns into an investment in future freedom. Each responsible decision today expands the opportunities available tomorrow. This approach changes repayment from a painful duty into a significant step toward improved independence and personal confidence.

You can see improvements in other aspects of your life as financial discipline becomes ingrained in your daily routine. Your capacity to save frequently, make prudent investments, and make deliberate purchases is strengthened by the patience you gain from regular payback. Greater resilience in the face of future hardships is encouraged by the confidence that comes with conquering financial difficulties. Every disciplined behavior supports the assumption that genuine development is produced via consistent dedication rather than flawless circumstances.

Ask yourself whether your present financial choices are improving your future freedom or limiting your future chances. Which financial commitment needs your immediate attention, and what doable steps can you take right now to lessen it? What needless spending habit could be turned toward enhancing your long-term financial security? How would your life alter if more of your income stayed available to support your future instead of your past? In order to go closer to long-term financial independence, what commitment are you willing to make today?

The willingness to take one responsible step and then go on to the next is the first step towards any significant accomplishment. Sudden achievement or good fortune do not lead to financial freedom. It is built through consistent discipline, thoughtful planning, and the determination to remain focused despite temporary challenges. With patience and self-assurance, keep putting these ideas into practice, knowing that each payment, prudent choice, and disciplined habit you make will improve the future you are building. Those who stay dedicated to meaningful activity long after initial motivation wanes are the ones who achieve lasting achievement. Every step you take will lessen needless obligations, expand worthwhile opportunities, and get you closer to a future characterized by self-assurance, security, freedom, and enduring financial serenity.

CHAPTER VII

Income Growth Opportunities

Career Skill Development

Career skill development is one of the most valuable investments a person can make because the ability to earn revenue is tightly tied to knowledge, experience, adaptability, and ongoing progress. Even while investing, saving, and budgeting are crucial components of financial success, these practices gain even more strength when they are accompanied by rising earning potential. Every new skill, improved ability, and expanded area of expertise creates opportunities for professional advancement and greater financial stability. Rather than viewing career development as a one-time achievement completed through formal education, successful individuals understand that learning is a lifelong process that strengthens both personal growth and long-term financial security.

As industries, technology, and customer expectations continue to shift, the modern workplace is changing quickly. Skills that were highly valuable a decade ago may require significant updates to remain competitive today. People who actively enhance their skills put themselves in a better position to adjust to shifting market demands. Rather than being afraid of change, they see it as a chance to learn more and become more valuable in their line of work. People who are open to lifelong learning are better equipped to adapt to changing work settings, new responsibilities, and developing technologies.

Understanding one's own strengths and pinpointing opportunities for development are the first steps in developing career skills. Every individual possesses unique talents, experiences, and interests that can be developed into valuable professional assets. Honest self-assessment allows people to recognize both their current abilities and the skills they need to strengthen in order to achieve future goals. This technique fosters intentional learning rather than haphazard effort. When development is guided by clear objectives, each new skill contributes directly to greater professional competence and improved career opportunities.

Technical abilities frequently offer the foundation for job growth since they demonstrate the ability to do specific activities effectively. Whether working in healthcare, education, technology, manufacturing, finance, creative sectors, or skilled professions, retaining current technical knowledge boosts both productivity and professional reputation. Individuals who remain informed about new tools, industry standards, and best practices become more valuable to employers and clients alike. Their experience allows them to address problems more efficiently while delivering higher quality work that supports long-term career advancement.

Equally important are interpersonal skills, which influence nearly every aspect of professional success. Effective communication, teamwork, active listening, conflict resolution, and emotional intelligence build relationships with coworkers, supervisors, clients, and business partners. Strong interpersonal abilities help individuals express ideas clearly, collaborate successfully, and build trust in professional settings. Because technical proficiency may not be sufficient to succeed in roles requiring leadership, customer interaction, or cooperative problem-solving, these attributes frequently set exceptional professionals apart.

Adaptability is another essential skill that contributes significantly to long-term financial success. Throughout a career, professional responsibilities, workplace expectations, and economic conditions frequently shift. People who welcome learning and are receptive to new ideas are better at adapting than people who are resistant to change. Adaptability allows people to acquire new competencies, accept evolving responsibilities, and remain productive even during periods of uncertainty. Because flexible professionals can continue to add value in the face of changing circumstances, this flexibility boosts career stability.

Time management also plays a critical role in career development. Professionals who manage their responsibilities well often accomplish more with less stress. Prioritizing important tasks, meeting deadlines, reducing distractions, and planning work efficiently improve both productivity and work quality. Effective time management makes it possible for people to learn more because they make more deliberate use of their free time. These behaviors eventually lead to increased opportunities for growth and increased professional dependability.

Problem-solving is another very valuable career ability that helps both professional achievement and financial prosperity. Every workplace has challenges that require critical analysis and practical answers. Individuals who approach problems with patience, creativity, and logical thinking often become trusted contributors within their organizations. Rather than avoiding unpleasant situations, they seek chances to enhance systems, resolve conflicts, and increase efficiency. Employers and clients constantly reward experts who bring meaningful solutions because their efforts create lasting improvements.

Developing leadership talents is beneficial even for persons who do not currently occupy management jobs. Leadership involves taking responsibility, demonstrating integrity, encouraging others, and contributing positively to organizational goals. Workers who exhibit initiative, dependability, and good judgment are frequently the best candidates for more responsibility. Leadership qualities boost professional reputation while opening doors to promotions, increased pay, and extended career options. True leadership focuses on serving others effectively while helping teams achieve shared success.

Continuous education is one of the most reliable methods for career skill development. Formal education, professional certifications, workshops, online courses, industry conferences, publications, and practical experience all help to develop knowledge. Successful people are aware that education never stops, even if a diploma or first training is over. Instead, they remain curious throughout their careers, recognizing that every new skill strengthens their ability to create value. This dedication to lifelong learning boosts self-esteem and enhances long-term employability.

Seeking constructive feedback is another important aspect of professional growth. Sincere feedback from managers, colleagues, mentors, or clients offers insightful information about strengths and areas for development. Individuals who welcome critique display humility and a genuine willingness to grow. Rather than considering criticism as personal failure, they treat it as information that directs future development. This commitment to develop consistently translates to higher performance and greater professional maturity.

By fostering chances for education, teamwork, and professional development, networking also promotes career advancement. Developing deep connections with coworkers, mentors, business leaders, and community members increases access to information and new prospects. Professional relationships often provide valuable advice, career guidance, referrals, and encouragement during periods of change. When networking is founded on sincere respect for one another and a desire to help rather than just pursuing one's own interests, it works best.

Development of career skills also calls for perseverance and self-control. Meaningful improvement rarely occurs without consistent effort over time. Acquiring new abilities frequently entails occasional setbacks, repeated efforts, and brief discomfort. Individuals who remain devoted despite these hurdles progressively gain competence that boosts both their professions and financial futures. Persistence transforms initial knowledge into practical competence while reinforcing confidence through repeated success.

Career development inevitably leads to financial gains since greater skill frequently opens doors to higher pay, more job security, promotions, consultancy work, entrepreneurial endeavors, or specialized professional services. Increased revenues often become a natural consequence of offering higher value, but they shouldn't be the main reason for learning. People who continuously develop their skills put themselves in a better position to contribute, which makes them desirable candidates for increased responsibility and professional progression.

Because professionals who prioritize long-term growth frequently approach money with similar discipline, career development also promotes stronger financial habits. They understand that spending money on training, credentials, equipment, or professional resources can increase earning potential and produce long-term benefits. This perspective encourages thoughtful spending that supports future success rather than focusing solely on immediate gratification. Viewing personal development as an investment boosts both professional progress and financial planning.

Another crucial component of a successful profession is maintaining one's physical and mental health. Productivity, creativity, decision-making, and professional relationships all depend on general wellness. People who prioritize getting enough sleep, maintain healthy routines, successfully handle stress, and take care of their physical fitness frequently perform better in difficult job environments. By boosting energy, focus, and perseverance during trying times, good health promotes long-term professional advancement.

Developing one's career skills also boosts confidence because each new skill increases one's ability to make a significant contribution. Confidence established by actual competence differs from overconfidence since it is underpinned by knowledge, experience, and consistent performance. Professionals who consistently improve their abilities speak more effectively, take on new problems with more confidence, and maintain composure under pressure. This self-assurance frequently fosters trust among coworkers, clients, and employers.

In the end, career skill development is a continuous dedication to both long-term financial success and personal brilliance. Greater professional value and more opportunities result from every lesson learned, every skill developed, and every obstacle surmounted. People who invest in continual improvement actively shape their own futures rather than depending just on outside factors to decide career results. They develop careers that can sustain long-term financial stability and personal fulfillment via lifelong learning, flexibility, discipline, solid relationships, and a dedication to delivering real value. Over time, these persistent efforts yield benefits that go well beyond higher earnings, such as increased self-assurance, a better professional reputation, more opportunities, and the satisfaction of knowing that success has been established via commitment, development, and the unwavering pursuit of excellence.

Multiple Income Streams

One of the best ways to improve long-term wealth and financial security is to create several sources of income. People who rely solely on one source of income may find themselves in a precarious financial situation when unforeseen circumstances arise. If there is only one source of income, household finances can be rapidly impacted by job loss, reduced working hours, company difficulties, health problems, or economic downturns. By strengthening financial resilience and expanding prospects for future expansion, generating many sources of income lowers this risk. Although creating several revenue streams takes time, work, and careful planning, the long-term advantages can go well beyond increased income. They offer more freedom, self-assurance, and the capacity to pursue worthwhile financial objectives with more assurance.

Many individuals believe that working much longer hours is necessary to make more money; however, having many sources of income does not always entail working longer hours. Rather, they entail broadening the sources of revenue. The principal source of income may continue to be a primary job, with supplementary income coming from consultancy, freelance work, small enterprises, investments, rental properties, digital products, royalties, or other options that fit one's hobbies and skill set. The goal is to build a financial structure that is less reliant on a single employer or economic situation rather than just becoming busier.

For many people, their primary career or occupation continues to be their initial and most significant source of income. A solid foundation for future financial success is provided by developing strong talents, upholding professional excellence, and pursuing career progression. Enhancing credentials through training, certifications, real-world experience, and ongoing study frequently boosts earning potential and creates new career prospects. In addition to generating resources that can be used to invest in creating other revenue streams, a solid main income covers everyday living needs.

One useful technique to generate extra revenue is through freelance employment. Outside of their regular jobs, those with particular abilities in writing, graphic design, programming, accountancy, consulting, photography, marketing, teaching, or many other disciplines can frequently offer services. People can increase their income while developing their professional networks and acquiring useful experience by freelancing. Freelancing can eventually become a substantial source of income or, if wanted, a full-time enterprise.

Another way to diversify your sources of income is to launch a small business. Many prosperous businesses start out as side projects that are progressively expanded alongside regular jobs. A company may concentrate on producing goods, services, instructional materials, or addressing certain issues in a community. In addition to requiring perseverance, meticulous planning, and persistent work, starting a business opens up revenue streams unrelated to hourly earnings. Genuine value-driven entrepreneurs frequently build companies that can generate steady, long-term profits.

Another significant source of financial growth is income from investments. Investments have the ability to produce returns over time through dividends, interest, capital appreciation, or other financial gains, in contrast to employment income, which typically depends on active effort. Even though there is always some risk associated with investing, careful preparation, diversification, and long-term discipline help minimize needless exposure. Investing consistently enables money to operate in tandem with individual effort, thereby leading to increased financial freedom.

Another possible extra source of income is rental revenue. Investors in residential or commercial real estate may benefit from potential long-term property appreciation in addition to regular rental payments. When handled properly, real estate ownership can boost an overall financial portfolio and generate consistent income, but it also necessitates thorough investigation, responsible administration, and financial planning. Investments in real estate should always be thoroughly assessed to make sure they complement available resources and long-term financial objectives.

Opportunities for earning money that were previously unattainable for the majority of people have increased because of digital technology. People can share their expertise and abilities with audiences worldwide through educational courses, electronic publications, digital templates, software applications, photography, music, online memberships, and other types of creative content. Digital products can continue to make money long after the primary labor is over, despite the fact that they sometimes need a substantial initial investment. The opportunity to profit from previously produced work highlights the need to fuse creativity with careful financial strategy.

Finding one's own abilities and potential is the first step in creating various revenue sources. Each person has special abilities, experiences, passions, or expertise that could be useful to others. While some people are very skilled in technical domains, others are excellent communicators, organizers, educators, artists, or leaders. Instead of trying to seek every potential source of income, identifying these talents enables people to concentrate on possibilities that align with their ability. Developing current abilities frequently yields greater outcomes than continuously looking for new opportunities.

Having several sources of income makes time management even more crucial. Careful scheduling is necessary for additional tasks to prevent disregarding one's major work obligations, family ties, or personal health. Gradually increasing income enables people to try new opportunities and keep a healthy balance without adding needless stress. In general, long-term consistency yields better outcomes than trying to expand quickly, which becomes challenging to maintain.

Even as income rises, financial discipline is still crucial. If spending increases at the same rate as earnings, wealth is not automatically created. The chance to increase savings, lower debt, increase investments, and improve financial security is one of the biggest benefits of having extra money. People can optimize the rewards of their labor and prevent needless lifestyle inflation by allocating a sizable amount of their new income toward long-term objectives. Earnings gains are most useful when they contribute to future financial stability rather than just funding increased spending.

The successful development of several revenue streams is supported by ongoing learning. Over time, markets, industries, technology, and consumer preferences all change. People who are dedicated to advancing their knowledge and abilities are better equipped to spot new possibilities and adjust to shifting conditions. Stronger long-term financial performance is a result of reading, participating in educational programs, learning from seasoned professionals, and obtaining real-world experience.

Another crucial quality while generating extra revenue is patience. Before generating significant financial results, many chances take months or even years. Professional reputations build gradually, businesses need time to draw in clients, and investments need time to expand. People who anticipate success right away frequently lose hope and give up on potential prospects too soon. Persistence and reasonable expectations are encouraged when extra money is seen as a long-term plan rather than a temporary fix.

Careful risk management is equally crucial. Diversification lessens reliance on a single source of income, but before investing a substantial amount of time or money, each option should be carefully considered. Reducing needless risk can be achieved by avoiding irrational pledges, thoroughly investigating opportunities, keeping emergency funds, and making small financial commitments. Instead of creating needless financial problems, responsible planning makes sure that initiatives to generate extra revenue increase overall financial stability.

The success of numerous revenue streams can also be greatly influenced by family support. Cooperation and understanding are fostered by open communication regarding shared tasks, time commitments, and financial goals. In order to improve both financial results and interpersonal ties, some families may even collaborate on economic endeavors or artistic endeavors. Long-term objectives are frequently simpler to accomplish when there is shared commitment, which also strengthens sound financial practices across the entire household.

Frequent assessment ensures that all sources of income continue to support long-term financial goals. People can concentrate their efforts on the most fulfilling prospects by reviewing profitability, time constraints, personal satisfaction, and future growth potential. While some sources of income might grow considerably, others might eventually be superseded by more favorable options. Being adaptable enables financial strategies to alter as opportunities and circumstances do.

Increasing both financial security and personal freedom is the ultimate goal of generating several sources of income. Every extra source of income increases the opportunity to accomplish worthwhile objectives while decreasing reliance on any one financial circumstance. Diversified income increases resilience in unpredictable times and boosts confidence while making future plans, whether through career development, freelancing, business ownership, investments, rental properties, or artistic endeavors. People can create a stronger financial foundation that supports long-term wealth, increased independence, and the capacity to make decisions based on personal values rather than financial constraints by combining careful planning, disciplined money management, ongoing education, and patient effort. Over time, having several sources of income turns into a potent demonstration of financial acumen, flexibility, and long-term vision in addition to being a source of extra money.

Increasing Earning Potential

Building long-term financial security requires increasing earning potential since doing so increases possibilities to save, invest, pay off debt, and accomplish important financial objectives. There is a realistic limit to how much spending can be cut, even though prudent money management is a crucial habit. However, income frequently has the capacity to increase as a result of ongoing education, enhanced performance, increased experience, and a readiness to take advantage of new chances. By generating extra resources that support both immediate demands and long-term prosperity, those who concentrate on growing their earning capacity strengthen their financial future. They actively look for ways to increase their capacity to add more value and get just remuneration for their contributions rather than relying only on their current income.

Developing useful talents is one of the best strategies to boost earning potential. People with skills and knowledge that solve issues, increase productivity, or support organizational success are rewarded in every profession. Professional value is increased by technical proficiency, communication skills, leadership traits, problem-solving abilities, and flexibility. People who engage in education stay competitive and set themselves up for more chances as sectors continue to change. Professionals can take on more challenging tasks, be eligible for promotions, and contribute at greater levels within their businesses thanks to continuous progress.

Increasing earning potential is also significantly influenced by education. Although formal education gives people the fundamental information they need to succeed in a variety of occupations, learning should continue even beyond graduation. Expanding expertise can be facilitated via self-directed study, industry conferences, workshops, online courses, seminars, and professional certifications.

The capacity to carry out worthwhile tasks and adjust to shifting work situations rises with each new skill learned. Employers and clients continually value the initiative and dedication that lifelong learning exhibits.

Another significant element that affects earning potential is experience. Real-world problem-solving skills, efficiency, confidence, and judgment are all enhanced by practical experience. People are frequently able to take on more responsibility and generate better outcomes as they gain experience. Because professionals learn from both successes and setbacks during their careers, experience also improves decision-making. Knowledge and real-world application combine to produce expertise, which grows in value over time.

Higher learning prospects are greatly influenced by developing a solid professional reputation. Employers, clients, and coworkers frequently trust people who continuously exhibit dependability, integrity, professionalism, and high-quality work. Opportunities for promotions, leadership positions, recommendations, consulting work, and long-term business partnerships are all made possible by a good reputation. Because businesses like to collaborate with people who regularly keep their word and favorably impact common objectives, trust is a significant asset. When fresh chances present themselves, professional credibility frequently becomes a deciding factor.

Another ability that has a direct impact on earning potential is effective communication. Professional connections are strengthened, and job performance is enhanced by the capacity to engage with others, listen intently, negotiate politely, and clearly explain concepts. Because they foster understanding and confidence among those they deal with, great communicators frequently go on to become more successful leaders, educators, salespeople, managers, and business owners. Effective communication enhances one's capacity to achieve favorable results and make a significant contribution in almost any type of work environment.

Increasing revenue also heavily depends on solving problems. People who recognize problems, create workable solutions, and enhance current procedures are valued by organizations. Professionals who constantly solve challenges become essential members of their teams rather than just finishing work as assigned. Both productivity and organizational success are increased by their capacity for critical thought and adapting to changing conditions. People who make significant improvements are frequently rewarded by employers because their effort adds value that lasts.

In today's ever-evolving economy, adaptability has become more and more crucial. Professionals must constantly adapt and welcome change due to new technologies, changing industry demands, and changing client expectations. People who oppose new advancements may eventually discover that their abilities are less useful. Because they can swiftly adapt to new responsibilities and opportunities, those who stay adaptable and receptive to learning set themselves up for long-term career advancement. By guaranteeing that professional abilities continue to be valuable in evolving situations, adaptability safeguards earning potential.

Increased income and career advancement are also greatly aided by networking. Chances to share expertise, find new career pathways, get mentorship, and discover job chances that might not be publicly posted are all made possible by professional partnerships. Genuine interest in other people, constant professionalism, and a desire to add value rather than pursue personal gain are necessary for developing meaningful friendships. Throughout a person's career, strong professional networks frequently serve as important sources of support.

Another trait that boosts earning potential is initiative. Leadership and dedication are demonstrated by those who voluntarily take on more duties, volunteer for difficult tasks, and look for chances to enhance performance at work. Because initiative shows a proactive mindset and a desire to go above and beyond what is required, employers often recognize it. Promotions, pay raises, increased responsibility, and increased professional recognition are frequently the results of this reputation over time.

Increased earning potential is also supported by entrepreneurial thinking, even for employees. Finding possibilities, coming up with innovative solutions to issues, increasing productivity, and concentrating on providing value are all components of entrepreneurial thinking. Workers who approach their jobs with this mentality frequently offer creative solutions that advance their companies. Eventually, some people use these abilities to start companies, provide consulting services, work as freelancers, or generate other sources of income that improve their financial security.

Creating a variety of revenue streams can lower financial risk and greatly boost total earning possibilities. Relying solely on one source of income can put you at risk if unforeseen events impact your job or business operations. Freelance work, consulting, investments, teaching, creative ventures, rental properties, and other options that fit one's hobbies and talents can all provide additional revenue. Having several sources of income increases financial flexibility and speeds up the achievement of long-term financial objectives.

Another crucial element in optimizing earning potential is time management. Effective time management frequently results in increased productivity, regular deadline compliance, and possibilities for further education or career advancement. Effective time management increases output without necessarily raising stress levels. Professionals who effectively manage their tasks frequently win the trust of clients and employers, which opens up new prospects and raises pay.

Career advancement is also aided by financial responsibility. Professionals who prudently handle their personal finances are less stressed, which enables them to concentrate better on their professional growth and productivity at work. They are more equipped to make investments in company prospects that boost earning potential, professional equipment, education, and certifications. Good money management gives you the freedom to take advantage of possibilities that might need short-term investments before they pay off in the long run.

Maintaining one's physical and mental health also affects one's ability to make money. Consistent productivity, creativity, resilience, and decision-making are all supported by good health. Professionals who take care of their health are frequently better able to manage challenging workloads, adjust to shifting tasks, and uphold healthy working relationships. By lowering the risk of burnout and fostering ongoing professional development, healthy habits improve long-term work performance.

As one's abilities, education, and experience develop, so does their confidence. Sincere confidence enables people to take on leadership roles, respectfully negotiate pay, pursue promotions, and investigate new professional options. Professionals are encouraged to acknowledge their worthwhile being dedicated to ongoing development when they have competence-based confidence. Stronger financial results and more job happiness are frequently the results of this balanced confidence.

Patience is also necessary to increase earning potential because significant career progress typically happens gradually. Rarely do promotions, pay raises, economic success, and professional recognition happen right away. Over many years, cumulative outcomes are produced by persistent improvement, continuous learning, and consistent work. People who persevere in the face of short-term setbacks are more likely to succeed in the long run because they recognize that gradual development, not instant gratification, is the key to long-term success.

Long-term earning potential is also significantly influenced by personal character. Integrity, honesty, dependability, and professionalism foster confidence, which enhances employment prospects. People who behave ethically and keep their word are regularly preferred by employers, clients, and business partners. Strong character fosters enduring relationships that lead to future possibilities and improves one's professional reputation.

Increasing earning potential ultimately comes down to becoming more valued by consistent development, responsible behavior, and significant contribution. Increased income comes from more than just working longer hours; it also comes from acquiring the information, abilities, experience, and character traits that enable people to handle more complex problems and add more value for others. People increase their professional and financial prospects through lifelong learning, flexibility, initiative, solid interpersonal connections, disciplined money practices, and steady personal growth. Over time, these efforts yield long-term benefits that go beyond higher earnings, such as enhanced self-assurance, job satisfaction, financial independence, and the ability to pursue worthwhile objectives. People build a solid basis for long-term prosperity and the capacity to make wiser financial decisions at every stage of life by considering personal and professional development as continuous investments rather than transient endeavors.

Expanding Financial Possibilities

Choosing to boost earning potential rather than just cutting expenses is one of the most empowering financial decisions a person can make. A solid financial foundation is produced by prudent planning, disciplined saving, and responsible spending, but long-term success is further enhanced when income increases in tandem with prudent financial practices. Because it promotes a proactive approach to financial advancement, this chapter is important. It shows that knowledge, abilities, inventiveness, and perseverance may provide chances that enhance both current stability and future prosperity, as opposed to viewing the existing situation as unchangeable. Every new skill acquired, every significant relationship formed, and every opportunity seized has the capacity to improve financial flexibility while creating previously unattainable opportunities. People start to grow when they realize that their ability to generate money is not fixed but may be enhanced by ongoing education and deliberate activity.

Applying the ideas discussed in this chapter alters people's perspectives on opportunities, employment, and education. They start to realize the importance of acquiring new skills, investigating novel concepts, and establishing several avenues for achieving financial security rather than viewing a job as the exclusive source of income. Because advancement is no longer reliant on a single salary or employment, confidence rises. People become more inclined to invest in their own growth when they realize that enhancing their skills frequently yields higher long-term benefits than buying transient luxuries. Because prospects are assessed based on future potential rather than current convenience, career selections become more strategic. Greater financial resilience benefits families because it offers security in erratic economic times. Increased confidence, adaptability, and the ability to make decisions based on long-term priorities are the outcomes in addition to improved earnings.

Future opportunities may be subtly limited if these concepts are disregarded. Without making significant adjustments to their skills or prospects, many people continue to carry out the same jobs, establish the same routines, and anticipate different financial outcomes. While income stays constant, growing living expenses may eventually lower purchasing power. Because unforeseen work changes, economic downturns, or personal situations can have a substantial impact on financial stability, relying solely on one source of income raises financial susceptibility. Opportunities for growth may also be lost if essential abilities or beneficial connections were never formed. The lack of ongoing development frequently leads to frustration—not because there are no opportunities, but rather because planning has not kept up with evolving conditions. Making the decision to not advance both personally and professionally could eventually prove to be more expensive than making the effort to do so.

Increasing financial options has far-reaching effects on actual life that go well beyond raising monthly income. Increased earning potential gives you more money to invest, save, support your family, donate to worthwhile causes, and get ready for retirement. It gives people more confidence to pursue education, travel, entrepreneurship, or professional changes. Because income growth increases flexibility when unforeseen expenses occur, financial stress frequently declines. Because several sources of income lessen reliance on a single source of funding, families experience increased security. Most significantly, ongoing development boosts self-esteem by demonstrating that progress is still achievable despite present conditions. Every new ability acquired turns into a precious asset that will continue to pay off for years to come.

By the end of this chapter, you will be able to assess your own strengths in order to pursue opportunities that fit your skills, values, and long-term financial goals; develop realistic action plans for creating multiple income sources that support long-term financial security; and identify practical opportunities for increasing your earning potential through skill development and strategic planning.

Take Melissa, for instance, who held an administrative role and thought her pay would never increase. Despite her prudent money management, she understood that improving her earning capacity was necessary for long-term financial advancement. She started attending inexpensive online classes in the evenings, which helped her develop her digital, project management, and communication skills. She offered to take on more duties at work, progressively showcasing her developing skills. She began providing small businesses with freelance administrative services on the weekends at the same time. She continued to build a profitable part-time business and received a promotion within a few years. Although her financial circumstances gradually improved, her confidence underwent the biggest change. She no longer saw herself as constrained by her situation. Through deliberate action and constant learning, she developed into someone who could create possibilities.

This lesson is exemplified via a short story. An experienced carpenter whose work was always in high demand was admired by a young craftsman. The young man was curious about his accomplishment and wondered if he had a unique gift that no one else had. Grinning, the carpenter gestured to a set of well-kept tools. He clarified that each year he developed a new ability, learned how to utilize a new tool, and practiced until quality became second nature. He kept learning new things while others continued to rely on the same restricted skills. He was eventually sought after by clients because he was able to resolve issues that others were unable to. The same idea applies to financial growth. Opportunities that are inaccessible to those who stop learning are created by people who consistently improve their skills.

The development of a wide-spreading tree serves as a helpful metaphor for increasing financial options. A tree starts out with a single, little trunk, but as time goes on, it grows numerous robust branches that extend in various directions. The tree will continue to develop even if one limb is injured during a storm since many other branches will still be strong and productive. Income can grow in a similar manner. It is similar to relying on a single branch to sustain the entire tree when one relies solely on one source. Many branches that offer more stability and resilience are created by developing new abilities, generating extra revenue streams, and fortifying professional ties. The more robust and varied those branches get, the better equipped the tree is to endure shifting seasons while still growing.

Use the Learn Build Expand Framework to start putting these concepts into practice right away. Start by determining your greatest abilities, passions, and experiences that could bring value for communities, clients, or companies. Make a list of the areas where you may improve to raise your earning potential, then choose one skill to work on over the next few months. Next, set aside time every week to learn through books, classes, workshops, real-world experience, or mentorship. As your skills develop, seek out chances to put them to use by taking on more responsibility, doing freelance work, consulting, coming up with small company ideas, or advancing your career. Maintain your professional connections by interacting with individuals who support development and impart insightful information. Review your progress, assess new opportunities, and modify your plan in response to evolving objectives or situations at the conclusion of each month. Continue doing this so that learning and opportunities become long-term habits rather than transient endeavors.

This framework's strength is its emphasis on ongoing development rather than instant perfection. Many people put off taking advantage of new chances because they think they need to be fully knowledgeable before starting. In actuality, significant development typically results from consistent learning coupled with real-world experience. Every new skill enhances current competencies and opens up new avenues for success in the future. Over time, little advancements add up to create opportunities that previously appeared unattainable.

Realizing that personal development frequently results in advantages beyond higher income is another crucial lesson. Gaining proficiency in communication, leadership, organization, creativity, technical knowledge, or problem-solving techniques boosts self-assurance in all spheres of life. These skills foster improved decision-making, strengthen bonds with others, and increase resilience in times of transition. One important outcome of a far more extensive process of personal development is financial prosperity. Because information and abilities continue to generate value long after they are obtained, investing in oneself continues to be one of the greatest returned investments you can make.

Increasing financial opportunities also requires patience. Seldom does meaningful growth occur overnight. It typically takes months or years of constant work to build promotions, profitable enterprises, professional recognition, and many revenue streams. Never assume that short-term setbacks equate to long-term failure. Every obstacle offers a fresh chance to hone skills, increase perseverance, and enhance tactics. Those who stay dedicated to their studies frequently find that one of their biggest long-term benefits is the experience they get throughout trying times.

Pursuing possibilities that are consistent with your principles and long-term goals is equally vital. Rather than taking the place of a meaningful life, financial development should enhance it. When more money leads to more freedom, better relationships, more well-being, and chances to impact others positively, it becomes most valued. Carefully selecting opportunities guarantees that financial success improves overall quality of life rather than causing needless stress or imbalance.

Consider whether you are devoting enough time to acquiring the abilities that will enhance your prospects in the future. Which skill could increase your earning potential the most over the coming years? What chance have you put off because you were unsure of your confidence or experience? If you regularly set aside time each week for professional development and learning, how would your financial future change? What doable action can you take now to increase your chances tomorrow?

Every long-lasting financial progress starts with the choice to expand beyond existing constraints. The knowledge, self-control, and decisions you make today will determine the opportunities you have tomorrow. Continue honing your skills with perseverance, curiosity, and resolve, realizing that each new skill and lesson you acquire will help you in the future. It doesn't need exceptional talent to advance. It calls for persistent work, intentional learning, and an openness to new opportunities. As you keep putting these ideas into practice, every new opportunity you take will lead to more financial assurance, better flexibility, long-term stability, and a future full of opportunities brought about by your own ongoing development and dedication.

CHAPTER VIII

Confident Investing Basics

Investment Fundamentals

The basis for creating long-term wealth is provided by investment fundamentals, which assist people in converting money into assets with the ability to increase in value over time. While earning and saving money are crucial financial practices, investing enables funds to contribute to future financial objectives by generating development prospects that go beyond merely retaining cash. Luck, speculation, or trying to forecast short-term market changes are not the foundation of successful investing. Rather, it relies on knowing the fundamentals of finance, being disciplined, handling risk sensibly, and staying dedicated to long-term goals. Those who gain a firm grasp of investment principles are better equipped to make deliberate choices that promote long-term financial stability.

Putting money into assets with the potential to grow in value or produce income over time is the main goal of investing. Investing concentrates on future gains by letting financial resources develop through appreciation, interest, dividends, rental income, or other types of return, as opposed to spending, which offers instant consumption. Every investment requires weighing potential benefits against potential dangers, thus thorough planning and knowledge are crucial components of the decision-making process. Knowing this balance enables people to approach investing with reasonable expectations rather than irrational aspirations of rapidly getting wealthy.

Understanding the connection between risk and return is one of the most crucial investing concepts. Generally speaking, investments with higher potential returns also carry a higher degree of risk and the potential for bigger losses. On the other hand, less risky investments frequently yield smaller returns. Knowing this link enables people to make investing decisions that align with their specific circumstances, financial objectives, and level of comfort with uncertainty. Careful investors concentrate on attaining suitable growth while safeguarding their long-term financial stability rather than aiming for the biggest potential return regardless of risk.

One of the biggest benefits for investors is time. Money has a greater chance of benefiting from long-term growth and compounding the longer it is invested. When investment profits start producing more profits of their own, compounding takes place, resulting in growth that quickens with time. Even though compounding's impacts might seem insignificant in the beginning, they frequently grow in importance as assets are held for longer periods of time. Early investment, even in modest sums, enables time to become a potent ally in achieving financial stability.

Generally speaking, consistency is more beneficial than trying to make big investments seldom. Regardless of shifting market conditions, people can progressively increase their investments by making consistent contributions. This methodical approach promotes long-term commitment and lessens the temptation to forecast the ideal time to invest. By seeing investment contributions as a continuous financial priority rather than an activity saved for occasions when additional money happens to be available, regular investing also aids in the development of sound financial habits.

Another crucial investment principle is diversification. Diversification entails distributing investments over a variety of assets, markets, and industries as opposed to concentrating all financial resources in a single venture. Because diverse assets frequently react differently to shifting economic conditions, this strategy lessens the impact of poor performance in any one area. While diversification helps build a more balanced investment portfolio that can withstand uncertain times while fostering long-term growth, it does not completely eliminate risk.

Prior to choosing any investment, it is crucial to comprehend one's own financial objectives. Different investment techniques are needed for different goals. While planning for retirement several decades in advance gives more time to pursue long-term growth opportunities, saving for a short-term purchase may require more stability and easier access to funds. Determining suitable investment options, time spans, and acceptable risk levels is aided by well-defined objectives. Without clear goals, investing choices could become erratic or impacted more by transient market feelings than by long-term strategy.

A key component of successful investing is patience. Financial markets inevitably go through phases of expansion and contraction. People who respond emotionally to every change in the market frequently make choices that are detrimental to their long-term success. Investors are often prevented from profiting from future recoveries by selling stocks during brief dips or continuously altering strategy depending on short-term news. Being patient reduces needless emotional decision-making and gives investments enough time to accomplish their goals.

Investment performance and emotional control are tightly related. Financial decisions are frequently influenced more by excitement and fear than by information or thoughtful consideration. Some investors grow overconfident and take needless risks while the market is performing well. Fear may promote selling investments at bad periods during market downturns. Instead of responding impulsively to transient events, developing emotional discipline enables people to stay focused on long-term goals. In addition to having sound financial knowledge, successful investment also requires the capacity to maintain composure and consistency in the face of shifting market conditions.

Making wise investing decisions throughout life is strengthened by financial education. Economic conditions fluctuate, markets shift, and new investment opportunities frequently appear. People who keep learning about investing are better able to assess opportunities sensibly and steer clear of needless risks. Reading credible financial resources, researching investment principles, and learning from experienced professionals help to improve long-term decision-making. Knowledge boosts confidence in responsible personal investment management while lowering uncertainty.

A comprehensive financial strategy should always be taken into consideration while making investment selections. Establishing emergency savings, handling high-interest debt sensibly, and keeping a realistic budget are all beneficial before making large investments. Because investments frequently perform best when left untouched for long periods of time, investing while financially unstable may put undue strain on investors amid unforeseen circumstances. Greater flexibility is made possible by a solid financial basis, which also keeps investment plans concentrated on long-term growth.

It's also critical to recognize the distinction between speculation and investing. Investing entails carefully assessing assets according to their long-term worth, sound financial principles, and reasonable expectations. Rapid price changes, transient opportunities, or hard-to-verify predictions are frequently the focus of speculation. Speculation includes a lot more risk and uncertainty, even though it can occasionally result in huge gains. In general, disciplined investment is more beneficial for people looking for long-term financial security than trying to make money through frequent short-term trading.

Regularly assessing the performance of investments promotes prudent financial management. Keeping an eye on portfolio performance helps guarantee that investments stay in line with evolving financial objectives and individual situations. Regular assessment, however, does not imply ongoing modification. Rather, it entails assessing whether investing strategies continue to support long-term goals and making deliberate modifications as needed. This well-rounded strategy promotes responsibility while discouraging needless trading based on transient market swings.

Healthy investing experiences are facilitated by controlling expectations. Investing usually builds wealth gradually rather than all at once. When results don't show up right away, unrealistic expectations frequently result in disappointment, annoyance, or bad financial choices. Recognizing that investments take time to provide significant returns promotes perseverance while highlighting the importance of regular contributions and long-term planning. Rather than a single exceptional opportunity, financial success is frequently the outcome of several years of disciplined investing.

Protecting investments through proper risk management remains equally crucial. Stronger long-term results can be achieved by avoiding undue concentration in any one asset, maintaining proper diversification, and routinely assessing financial goals. Responsible investors know that protecting capital is equally as vital as pursuing growth because major losses need substantial future profits merely to recover. Making balanced decisions minimizes needless exposure to preventable dangers and promotes sustained financial advancement.

Investment strategy may also need to be modified when individual circumstances change. Investment decisions are influenced by a number of factors, including career development, marriage, family responsibilities, company ownership, retirement preparation, and shifting financial goals. Investment portfolios are regularly reviewed to make sure they continue to meet present objectives while adjusting to new possibilities or responsibilities. Flexibility enables financial plans to change without compromising the fundamentals of long-term, disciplined investing.

In the end, investment principles give people the information and self-assurance they need to increase their wealth over time gradually. Finding ideal opportunities and forecasting every market movement are not the goals of investing. It involves making well-informed choices, exercising patience, handling risk sensibly, and continuously allocating funds for long-term expansion. People develop investment habits that promote long-term prosperity and financial independence through disciplined saving, careful diversification, ongoing education, emotional control, and frequent assessment. Every carefully thought-out investment is a pledge to future stability, enabling today's prudent choices to become tomorrow's financial prospects. These steady routines build a strong basis for long-term prosperity and the ability to confidently and steadily pursue worthwhile life goals.

Managing Investment Risk

Discovering opportunities with the best possible returns is just one part of being a successful investor. Just as important is being aware of and doing what you can to mitigate the dangers that come with any financial decision. Due to the inherent unpredictability in all assets, it is impossible to remove investment risk entirely. Planning ahead, making educated decisions, and maintaining consistent financial habits can help control risk. People who are good at balancing risk and reward are more likely to keep more of what they earn and even grow it over time. Successful investors don't chase short-term gains or react emotionally to market fluctuations; instead, they focus on developing methods that enable them to persevere through times of uncertainty while staying dedicated to their long-term goals.

Realizing that various investments entail varying degrees of uncertainty is a crucial part of managing investment risk. Having cash on hand is a safe bet, but it could see its value erode due to inflation. Bonds are a safer investment than stocks because of their more consistent yields, but they may not increase as quickly. Although stock prices are often volatile, they also have the potential to provide large gains over long periods of time. Investing in commodities, real estate, and other alternative assets comes with its own set of risks and potential benefits.

Investors may better tailor their portfolios to their financial objectives, time horizons, and level of comfort with uncertainty when they have a firm grasp of these traits, as opposed to letting their emotions or trend following dictate their selections.

One of the most effective ways to lower investment risk is to diversify. The goal of diversification is to reduce the risk of an investor's capital being overly concentrated in any one business, market, or asset class. Because gains from other assets can sometimes cancel out losses, this strategy helps mitigate the effects of underperformance in one area. Although it is impossible to shield a portfolio from risk completely, diversification can lessen the impact of any one adverse event. Consistent diversification builds stronger financial foundations that can better weather economic storms.

When it comes to lowering investment risk, time is also of the essence. The ups and downs of market expansion and recovery are inevitable. Inexperienced investors may sell valuable stocks during short-term downturns out of fear of losing more money. Stock market fluctuations are common and frequently short-lived, as any investor worth their salt can tell you when you look at the big picture. Many investors have profited from future recoveries by staying involved during bad times. Emotional decisions made in times of anxiety can lead to needless financial losses, making patience a crucial risk management technique.

Effective risk management is greatly enhanced by well-defined financial objectives. Those who have a clear goal in mind for their savings can make more informed financial decisions. With decades to ride out market downturns, retirees saving for the future may opt for investments with higher growth potential. Conversely, a homebuyer with a few years to save for a down payment would favor more cautious choices that put a premium on preserving cash rather than chasing gains. To lessen the likelihood that unneeded risks may derail the attainment of critical life objectives, it is wise to align investing strategies with financial deadlines.

An investor's capacity to deal with uncertainty is enhanced by knowledge and ongoing learning. Because of the dynamic nature of economies, industry, and technology, financial markets are in a perpetual state of flux. An investor's ability to spot opportunities and red flags improves when they make it a habit to educate themselves. Investments are impacted by interest rates, purchasing power is impacted by inflation, and market success can be impacted by global events. Consistent learning lessens the need to guess and boosts self-assurance when handling money in times of uncertainty.

Effective risk management also requires emotional discipline. Investing decisions are frequently driven more by greed and fear than by logic and reason. Exuberance during fast-rising markets could lead investors to buy assets at exorbitant prices, just because it seems like everyone else is making money. As a result of panic, some investors may sell high-quality assets at steep losses when the market falls. Investors who have trained themselves to control their emotions are better able to make long-term decisions based on solid plans. Consistency and the absence of impulsive acts that might derail long-term financial gains are fostered by sticking to a stated investment strategy.

Keeping a healthy risk-reward ratio requires regular portfolio evaluations. Investment returns cause a slow but steady shift in the initial distribution of funds. There is an increase in total risk if a high-performing investment becomes a bigger portion of the portfolio than planned. By modifying investments on a periodic basis to keep exposure constant across various asset classes, rebalancing returns the portfolio to its intended allocation.

Investors can stay aligned with their long-term goals and avoid becoming too reliant on any one investment by following this rigorous method.

Recognizing one's own level of comfort with danger is also crucial. When it comes to money, everyone is more or less at ease with ambiguity. Even minor changes might cause a great deal of anxiety for certain investors, while others are able to maintain composure throughout steep market drops. During times of market volatility, it is easy to make poor financial choices when one's emotional tolerance is too high. Investors can adopt methods they can confidently maintain through changing market conditions by honestly assessing themselves. Instead of continual worry, a well-designed financial plan should inspire confidence.

Investment risk can be mitigated by keeping a sufficient emergency fund. If they don't have an emergency fund, investors may have to sell their long-term investments during bad market conditions due to unexpected medical bills, job loss, or family problems. While short-term problems are handled, investments can stay put in an emergency fund, giving you financial flexibility. By keeping emergency funds separate from long-term investments, wealth creation plans are safeguarded against being derailed by immediate financial obligations.

A key component of risk management is accepting the fact that being completely cautious might lead to monetary difficulties in and of itself. Even though capital is safe in the near run with an extremely cautious strategy, it might not produce enough growth to counter inflation in the long run. The purchase power of savings gradually decreases as prices rise, lowering their true value. Finding a happy medium between the two competing demands of stability and growth is essential for successful investment. To keep buying power while reducing needless exposure to excessive risk, carefully choose investments that match long-term goals.

The key to being a successful investor is being able to adjust to changing market conditions without losing sight of your long-term goals. The financial markets are sensitive to a wide range of factors, including interest rates, inflation, new technology, government regulations, and world events. Disciplined investors put less emphasis on trying to anticipate every move in the market and more on diversifying their holdings, checking in on their progress often, and making changes to their strategies only when their objectives or financial situations change. With this methodical strategy, you can build wealth steadily and lessen the chances of making rash, emotionally driven judgments.

Avoiding uncertainty isn't as important as effectively preparing for it when it comes to managing investment risk. An investment strategy that can endure changing market conditions is one that is well-planned, diverse, patient, constantly learning, emotionally disciplined, and has consistent financial habits. Those who put their money where their mouth is and accept risk as a necessary evil are in a better position to seize opportunities while minimizing losses. In the long run, this methodical strategy promotes financial security, protects assets, and enables the consistent development necessary to attain substantial financial success.

Growing Long Term

Growing wealth over the long term is a process predicated on patience, consistency, discipline, and deliberate decision-making rather than sudden financial successes. Promises of quick success or easy wealth draw a lot of people, but long-term financial security is nearly always the result of consistent behaviors developed over many years. While every needless financial error can impede growth, every prudent financial choice made today creates opportunity for the future. Long-term growth is not about making perfect decisions every time but about developing habits that consistently move financial resources in a positive direction. People who grasp this idea are more likely to stick with their objectives in the face of short-term setbacks or shifting financial circumstances.

One of the most significant features of long-term financial prosperity is having a clear vision of the future. Without a purposeful destination, financial decisions typically become reactive rather than intentional. A long-term vision provides direction by recognizing what financial success genuinely means on a personal level. For one person, it may mean obtaining financial independence, while another may focus on providing educational opportunities for children, building a comfortable retirement, starting a business, supporting charity organizations, or leaving a financial legacy for future generations. Defining these objectives gives reason behind every saving, investing, and spending action, making it simpler to remain disciplined over time.

Consistency is often more crucial than intensity when pursuing long-term growth. Large financial achievements are frequently the product of innumerable modest activities repeated routinely rather than rare remarkable efforts. Saving a portion of every pay check, making consistent investment contributions, paying bills on time, limiting wasteful spending, and consistently developing financial knowledge may sound straightforward individually, but combined they yield tremendous benefits over many years. Regardless of short-term setbacks, people who concentrate on upholding these practices get momentum that progressively improves their financial situation.

Patience remains one of the best benefits in generating long-term wealth. Financial development rarely comes in a straight line, and real gains may need years of diligent labor before becoming fully obvious. Because they anticipate instant benefits for prudent financial behavior, many people grow disappointed. But long-term growth requires giving investments time to grow, savings to build up, careers to advance, and financial habits to solidify. Those who exercise patience are more likely to reap the benefits of steady advancement while avoiding rash decisions motivated by immediate disappointment.

Long-term financial growth is significantly influenced by compounding. Future earnings start generating more earnings when investments and savings provide returns that are reinvested rather than spent. This process speeds up financial growth over long stretches of time in ways that may appear small at first but rise in importance over time. Higher returns are simply one aspect of compounding's inherent strength; another is the discipline needed to keep money invested for a long time. The benefits of starting early and sticking with it are frequently greater than trying to invest more money much later in life.

Long-term financial success is intimately correlated with prudent spending management. Every dollar spent needlessly is a lost chance to invest, save, or get ready for the future. This does not imply giving up all pleasurable activities or living under continual financial constraints. Rather than relying on fleeting impulses, it entails making deliberate spending choices that represent individual priorities. Individuals who discriminate between significant purchases and wasteful consumption conserve larger financial resources for possibilities that support sustainable growth.

Avoiding excessive debt promotes long-term financial growth by protecting future revenue. When borrowing money for non-essential goods, obligations are frequently created that last long after the initial satisfaction has faded. The amount of money available for saves, investments, education, or other important financial objectives is diminished by interest payments. Financial flexibility is increased by prudent debt management and avoiding needless borrowing, which frees up resources for future prosperity rather than previous spending choices.

Since financial knowledge changes over the course of a person's life, ongoing education promotes long-term growth. Over time, human circumstances, technological advancements, investment opportunities, and economic conditions all change. People who stay dedicated to their studies are better able to adjust and make wise financial choices. Long-term financial confidence is strengthened by reading financial literature, learning about investment principles, honing professional abilities, and gaining practical experience. Knowledge enables people to spot possibilities and steer clear of many typical financial blunders.

Another significant factor in long-term financial success is career advancement. Greater earning potential is frequently the result of improving professional skills, obtaining worthwhile experience, going back to school, and growing as a leader. Increased savings, faster investments, quicker debt reduction, and readiness for future financial obligations are all made possible by higher income. But income increase on its own is insufficient. Instead of greater consumption, long-term wealth is created when more wages are paired with prudent money management.

Long-term financial stability is further strengthened by creating several sources of income. Because unforeseen changes can have a substantial impact on financial stability, relying just on one source of income makes one vulnerable. Greater freedom and lower financial risk are provided by additional income from freelancing, business ownership, investments, rental properties, or artistic endeavors. In addition to generating extra funds for investments and savings, diversified sources of income can speed up long-term financial progress without relying just on one line of work.

Keeping an emergency reserve safeguards long-term development in the event of unforeseen circumstances. Medical bills, house repairs, car upkeep, brief unemployment, and other financial surprises are unavoidable in life. People could have to stop making investments, take on more debt, or give up on long-term goals if they don't have emergency reserves. A solid financial reserve makes it possible to handle difficulties without seriously impairing long-term objectives. In times of uncertainty, this consistency reduces emotional financial decision-making while boosting confidence.

Frequent financial evaluations guarantee that long-term strategies stay in line with evolving conditions. As occupations advance, families expand, responsibilities rise, and retirement draws near, personal priorities inevitably change throughout life. Examining spending patterns, investment plans, savings targets, and budgets enables careful modifications while maintaining general direction. Maintaining flexibility without losing sight of more general financial goals is more important for long-term success than strict adherence to antiquated strategies.

Maintaining long-term progress requires emotional self-control. There are times of uncertainty in financial markets, the state of the economy, and individual situations. Decisions that impede long-term success are frequently motivated by fear, enthusiasm, frustration, or impatience. Instead of reacting emotionally, those who maintain composure in the face of brief setbacks are more likely to continue making deliberate financial decisions.

People with emotional resilience are able to stay focused on long-term objectives in the face of temporary setbacks or diversions.

Financial growth is also influenced by healthy relationships. Families that are open about their financial priorities are more cooperative, accountable, and supportive of one another. When a couple plans together, they are more likely to make consistent financial decisions and avoid needless arguments over saving or spending. By educating future generations to handle money sensibly and responsibly, teaching children sound financial practices expands the advantages of long-term planning.

By promoting contentment with steady growth rather than continual comparison with others, gratitude enhances long-term financial success. People who value their accomplishments are less inclined to engage in wasteful spending to keep up appearances or compete with shifting societal norms. Gratitude encourages deliberate decision-making while keeping financial resources concentrated on important personal objectives rather than transient outside influences.

Since setbacks are unavoidable on any long-term endeavor, resilience is equally crucial. Businesses face difficulties, employment possibilities shift, investment markets fluctuate, and unforeseen costs arise. People are better equipped to keep going on if they see these occurrences as transient challenges rather than irreversible failures. Every obstacle offers a chance to hone discipline, increase financial literacy, and better future tactics. The capacity to bounce back from setbacks is more important for long-term success than completely avoiding challenges.

In the end, accumulating wealth over time is the outcome of numerous deliberate choices made continuously throughout life. Finding a single exceptional investment opportunity or relying just on income does not decide it.

Rather, disciplined saving, careful planning, smart investing, reasonable spending, ongoing education, emotional control, and unshakable dedication to worthwhile objectives are the keys to long-term financial success. Every little financial choice adds to a bigger picture that gets stronger over time. In addition to increasing their wealth, people who are patient, flexible, and maintain prudent financial practices also get more independence, security, and self-assurance. Long-term growth transcends financial success through consistent advancement and deliberate action. It turns into a way of life that fosters long-term success, worthwhile chances, and a future based on steadiness, fortitude, and deliberate everyday choices.

Planting Seeds Of Wealth

It takes more than just earning, saving, and carefully controlling spending to create long-term financial security. It also necessitates letting money operate profitably over time. Many people put in years of hard labor to earn every dollar they get, but they never allow their money to grow in tandem with their own efforts. This chapter is important because it presents a perspective that goes beyond short-term financial need and concentrates on generating long-term opportunities. Predicting the ideal time or pursuing rapid returns are not the goals of wise investing. Making deliberate choices, being patient, controlling risk, and letting time become one of your biggest financial advantages are all important. Every investment is a decision to allocate resources from today to prospects that could lead to prosperity in the future. Investing is no longer an activity motivated by uncertainty or emotion, but rather a useful tool for achieving financial independence when done with knowledge and discipline.

By putting the ideas discussed in this chapter into practice, people's perspectives on their financial future are altered. They start to realize that wisely allocated resources might progressively generate further financial growth rather than depending exclusively on employment income. When financial decisions are made with information rather than speculation or fear, confidence rises. The need for instant gratification is replaced by patience, which enables deliberate tactics to yield significant long-term outcomes. People are more inclined to thoroughly research options, assess any dangers, and stick with their commitments during brief shifts in the market. When investments start to support objectives like retirement, education, business expansion, or long-term family stability, financial planning becomes more comprehensive. This methodical technique reduces the emotional decision-making that frequently results in needless losses while promoting steady growth.

Even when present finances seem steady, disregarding these rules could have serious long-term repercussions. As living expenses fluctuate over time, money that is idle and unused progressively loses purchasing value. If people don't learn about investing, they might rely solely on earned income for the rest of their life, which would limit their flexibility in the future and their chances of building long-term wealth. Eventually, some people might invest without doing enough study, basing their choices on hearsay, excitement, or fear rather than thorough investigation. These emotional decisions frequently result in unsatisfactory outcomes that deter further involvement. Therefore, failing to grasp responsible investing could result in lost chances or needless financial errors. Both results postpone advancements that could have been made with persistent action and patient learning.

Thoughtful investment has far more practical benefits than just raising account balances. Because resources keep increasing over time, it offers more assurance when making retirement plans. Diversified long-term planning gives families more financial security. Parents are better equipped to assist their children's academic objectives. Because investments progressively improve their total financial position, people have more flexibility when pursuing job changes, launching enterprises, or reacting to unforeseen possibilities. More significantly, investing promotes long-term thinking, which affects all facets of financial decision-making. People start weighing options based on their future worth rather than just their present rewards. This viewpoint encourages more deliberate use of financial resources while bolstering discipline.

By the end of this chapter, you will be able to assess investment opportunities more confidently by using careful research and long-term thinking, create a workable investment strategy that strikes a balance between growth and prudent risk management, and establish dependable routines that enable patience, self-control, and well-informed decision-making to support long-term financial advancement.

Think about Samuel's experience, who thought investing required substantial sums of money and specialized skills. He put off learning for a number of years since he believed it was out of his reach. He ultimately made the decision to educate himself by reading reputable financial publications, going to educational seminars, and talking to seasoned investors. He started making regular small contributions to varied long-term investments that were suitable for his financial circumstances rather than taking on hazardous investments that promised unrealistic returns. Because he saw the benefits of long-term planning, he stayed dedicated even when market prices momentarily dropped. His investment portfolio had increased significantly over the years thanks to steady contributions and careful discipline. In retrospect, Samuel saw that starting small and early proved to be considerably more beneficial than waiting for ideal conditions that never materialized.

This lesson is exemplified via a short story. An experienced farmer was questioned by a novice orchard owner about how he was able to consistently harvest large amounts of fruit while others battled with uneven yields. Grinning, the farmer clarified that he never evaluated his orchard based on a single season. He meticulously prepared the soil, irrigated the trees regularly, chose healthy seeds, shielded them from needless harm, and gradually let nature take its course. Every season added to the orchard's strength, while some saw faster growth than others. The same idea applies to financial investing. Impatience and continual change seldom produce meaningful outcomes. They grow as a result of careful planning, constant attention, and faith in the long-term process.

Planting a forest instead of gathering firewood is a helpful metaphor for investing. Although it offers instant warmth, firewood must be refilled after a short while. A forest takes time to grow, but once it is established, it continues to yield advantages for many years. Every well-considered investment is like planting a new, healthy tree. The forest can gradually grow until it offers long-lasting strength and resilience with time, regular maintenance, and careful management. People who are always looking for instant gratification frequently use today's resources without generating prospects for the future. A forest that can sustain future generations is progressively created by those who patiently plant and care for financial trees.

Use the Learn Evaluate Invest Review Framework to start putting these concepts into practice right away. Prior to investing in any possibility, start by improving your understanding of finance. Learn about various financial possibilities, familiarize yourself with potential risks and benefits, and study trustworthy educational materials.

Next, carefully assess each possibility by taking into account your entire financial status, investment timeframe, personal risk tolerance, and financial goals. Don't base your choices only on fear, excitement, or promises of exceptionally high profits. Instead of trying to forecast ideal market conditions, start making regular contributions in accordance with your financial plan once you have chosen the right investments. Lastly, evaluate your investing success on a frequent basis without becoming emotionally upset by short-term swings. Only make deliberate changes when your long-term plan, life circumstances, or financial objectives call for it. Throughout your financial journey, keep going through this process, letting patience and discipline direct your choices.

This framework's strength is its focus on planning rather than forecasting. Knowing exactly what the markets will do tomorrow is rarely a prerequisite for successful investing. Rather, it relies on gaining knowledge, making good choices, controlling risk, and sticking to a well-thought-out plan. Because they comprehend the rationale behind their choices rather than responding to fleeting headlines or emotional pressure, people who adopt these behaviors frequently feel more confident.

Realizing that patience frequently turns into one of the biggest financial benefits available to any investor is another important lesson. Consistent contributions, long-term growth, and compounding impacts can all coexist over time. A lot of individuals don't realize how tiny, consistent investments can grow into substantial wealth over time. Instead of recognizing the remarkable effects of persistent discipline, they concentrate on quick outcomes. Each donation serves as a new seed for wealth in the future. Long-term growth is more likely the earlier this process starts.

It is equally crucial to keep in mind that risk management is always a part of prudent investing. Since every investment entails some degree of uncertainty, careful diversification, continual learning, and reasonable expectations are crucial components of long-term success. Never let confidence turn into overconfidence. Sensible investors maintain their curiosity, keep learning, and recognize that safeguarding financial assets is just as crucial as expanding them. Stability is produced by balanced decision-making in both advantageous and difficult market circumstances.

Additionally, investing promotes a more comprehensive view of financial success. People start realizing the worth of assets that continue to function long after the initial effort has been finished, as opposed to gauging success just by current income. In every aspect of life, this change promotes more patience, deliberate preparation, and responsible financial conduct. It reaffirms the idea that long-term prosperity is developed gradually by regular, consistent efforts over a long period of time.

Consider whether your present financial practices enable your money to expand in proportion to your effort. In order to make more confident financial judgments in the future, what investment knowledge do you still need to acquire? Instead of waiting for perfect conditions, which long-term objective could be strengthened by starting consistent investing today? If you stayed patient and dedicated to a careful investment approach for many years, how might your future financial security change? What doable steps can you take this week to start sowing the financial seeds that will help you in the future?

Every long-lasting financial legacy starts with a single, deliberate choice that is followed by years of steadfast dedication. Rarely are shortcuts and good fortune the only ways to become wealthy. It develops by knowledge, perseverance, disciplined behavior, and the capacity to look beyond short-term gains. Continue to fortify your financial future by approaching each investment choice with discernment, readiness, and assurance. Let time be your greatest ally instead of your worst challenge. Every choice you make will improve the future you are building and move you closer to a life characterized by self-assurance, opportunity, resiliency, and long-term financial success as you continue to sow the seeds of sustainable prosperity through thoughtful planning and responsible action.

CHAPTER IX

Lasting Financial Protection

Insurance Essentials

A solid financial plan must include insurance because it shields people and families from unforeseen circumstances that may otherwise result in severe financial hardship. Increasing income, saving regularly, and making prudent investments are not the only ways to build wealth. Additionally, it involves safeguarding the financial advancements that have already been made. Financial difficulties brought on by unforeseen illnesses, accidents, property damage, natural disasters, or the loss of a family income can take years to resolve. By lessening the impact of these unanticipated catastrophes, insurance adds a layer of financial safety. Knowing the fundamentals of insurance enables people to make well-informed choices that promote long-term financial stability while lowering needless financial risk.

The fact that insurance is intended to manage risk rather than totally remove it is one of the most crucial ideas to comprehend. There are many unknowns in life that no one can fully foresee. Even while responsible living and cautious planning lower many risks, some things are still out of one's control. In order for those who suffer insured losses to obtain financial support when necessary, insurance operates by enabling a large number of people to make comparatively little contributions through recurring premiums. People who have significant financial setbacks that might normally be challenging to handle on their own might recover more rapidly thanks to this collaborative method.

Instead of being seen as an investment meant to make money, insurance should be seen as a type of financial protection. Some people are hesitant to buy insurance because they think they won't ever need it. But the security insurance offers before a claim is ever filed is what really makes it valuable. Families and individuals can concentrate on healing rather than stressing about how to handle high costs when they know that financial assistance is accessible during trying times. One of the biggest advantages of keeping insurance protection is frequently the peace of mind that results from having the right coverage.

Even for healthy people, medical costs can add up, making health insurance one of the most crucial types of financial security. Many families may not be able to cover the costs of unexpected illnesses, injuries, operations, or long-term therapies with their personal funds alone. Health insurance improves access to essential therapy while lowering the cost of medical care. By preventing medical costs from interfering with savings, investments, or other financial objectives, maintaining sufficient health coverage safeguards both long-term financial stability and physical well-being.

Another crucial factor is life insurance, especially for people who have financial obligations to dependents or family members. The main goal of life insurance is to support loved ones financially in the event that the insured person dies suddenly. During a challenging time of transition, these payments may be used to support daily living expenditures, pay off existing debts, replace lost income, or finance educational costs. Because it shows a dedication to safeguarding the future well-being of family members who rely on continuous financial support, selecting the right life insurance represents sensible financial planning.

Financial asset protection is another important function of property insurance. Homes, cars, and personal items are frequently the result of years of diligent planning, saving, and hard labor. If these assets are not sufficiently protected, significant financial losses could be caused by fires, storms, theft, accidents, and other unforeseen calamities. By lowering the financial effects of loss or damage, property insurance enables people to replace or repair valuables without using up all of their personal money. Long-term wealth building initiatives are supported as financial progress is maintained through the protection of important assets.

Another crucial type of security that is occasionally disregarded is disability insurance. Many people prioritize safeguarding tangible assets while undervaluing the significance of safeguarding their capacity to make money. A major sickness or injury can make it impossible for a person to work, either temporarily or permanently, which lowers the amount of money required to cover daily expenses. When qualified medical conditions make employment impossible, disability insurance helps reimburse a portion of lost income. Since steady income underpins almost every facet of financial security, protecting earning capacity is crucial.

Rather than buying every policy offered, selecting the right insurance necessitates a thorough assessment of individual circumstances. Age, family responsibilities, income, assets, occupation, health, and financial objectives are some of the variables that affect insurance needs. A young person starting a job could need different coverage than someone raising children or getting ready to retire. Reviewing insurance requirements on a regular basis guarantees that coverage stays in line with evolving life situations. In order to offer suitable levels of protection, insurance coverage should change as financial obligations do.

Another crucial component of good insurance management is comprehending policy information. Before buying insurance, people should spend some time learning about coverage limits, exclusions, deductibles, waiting periods, and claim procedures. It is easier to avoid misconceptions when financial support is most required if you know exactly what is covered. Carefully reading policy documents and asking questions when needed promotes informed decision-making while lowering the possibility of unpleasant surprises down the road.

When choosing insurance coverage, affordability should also be taken into account. While minimal coverage may expose people to large financial losses, purchasing excessive coverage beyond actual needs may put needless strain on monthly expenditures. People can appropriately manage insurance costs while retaining significant financial security when they choose a balanced level of protection. Along with savings, investments, debt management, and daily living costs, insurance payments should be included in the overall financial plan.

Keeping an emergency fund in addition to insurance improves overall financial readiness. Even if insurance covers a lot of important risks, personal savings may still be needed for some costs like deductibles, unprotected services, or brief financial setbacks. While insurance covers greater insured losses, emergency reserves offer instant financial flexibility. When combined, these two financial tools strengthen the safety net and enable people to deal with unforeseen difficulties more skillfully without substantially depending on debt.

Long-term wealth preservation is another benefit of insurance. It frequently takes years of diligent saving, investment, and cautious money management to achieve financial security. Resources that took decades to accumulate could be depleted by a single unforeseen incident in the absence of sufficient protection. Insurance lessens the impact of high unforeseen costs, protecting these financial accomplishments. Insurance enables long-term financial planning to proceed more smoothly rather than compelling them to sell investments or take out retirement funds.

The confidence that insurance fosters is another significant advantage. Stress is frequently brought on by financial uncertainty because people are concerned about how unforeseen circumstances may impact their family and financial prospects. Reassurance that suitable precautions have been made for numerous frequent dangers is provided by appropriate insurance coverage. Without continually worrying about financial catastrophe from unforeseen circumstances, this confidence enables people to concentrate on professional development, family duties, personal growth, and financial preparation.

Periodically examining policies is another aspect of responsible insurance administration. When a person gets married, has children, advances in their job, owns a home, retires, or grows their business, their circumstances change. Insurance requirements are frequently impacted by these changes. Frequent reviews find ways to modify protection or cut wasteful expenses while ensuring that current coverage is still suitable. Maintaining up-to-date insurance plans promotes long-term security and financial efficiency.

Avoiding needless insurance purchases is similarly crucial. Although protection is important, not every policy offers significant advantages to every person. Thorough assessment aids in separating necessary coverage from optional items that might not be in line with individual financial preferences. Making careful decisions guarantees that insurance resources are allocated to safeguard the biggest financial risks while keeping money for investments, savings, and other crucial objectives.

Additionally, by encouraging planning rather than reaction, insurance promotes responsible financial conduct. People acknowledge that uncertainty is a normal aspect of life and make appropriate preparations rather than expecting that unforeseen issues never arise. Beyond insurance, this proactive approach permeates other aspects of financial planning, such as investment management, budgeting, emergency savings, and retirement planning. Increased resilience and more assured financial decision-making are fostered by preparing for possible obstacles.

Understanding the fundamentals of insurance ultimately comes down to safeguarding financial advancement via careful planning and prudent risk management. Insurance is an important safety net that helps people and families recover from unforeseen circumstances without compromising long-term financial objectives. Insurance becomes a crucial basis for long-term financial security through careful assessment of individual needs, suitable coverage selection, frequent policy reviews, and integration with more comprehensive financial planning.

It enables people to preserve the riches they have worked so hard to accumulate while safeguarding their income, health, property, and loved ones. People build more confidence, stronger financial resilience, and a more secure future backed by preparedness, responsibility, and prudent daily financial decisions when they acknowledge insurance as a crucial part of a balanced financial plan rather than an unnecessary expense.

Protecting Valuable Assets

Since achieving financial success involves more than just earning, saving, and investing money, protecting valued assets is crucial to developing and maintaining long-term prosperity. If wealth accumulated over many years is not shielded against needless risks, it may be diminished or even lost. In addition to cash and investments, valuable assets include homes, businesses, cars, personal belongings, retirement funds, intellectual property, professional abilities, and even the capacity to generate revenue. Every asset is a representation of time, work, discipline, and sacrifice, so safeguarding it is equally as crucial as its development. People who comprehend this idea form sound financial practices that protect what they have established and more confidently position themselves for future chances.

The ability to make money is one of a person's most valued assets. Earning potential is influenced by professional expertise, real-world experience, technical proficiency, inventiveness, and diligent work habits. Maintaining physical and mental health, engaging in ongoing education, and adjusting to evolving industries and technology are all necessary to safeguard this asset. When employment prospects or economic conditions change, those with skills that are still relevant can continue to make money. Financially successful people see lifetime learning as a continuing investment in one of their greatest assets rather than as something that ends after formal schooling.

Maintaining financial stability also heavily depends on one's health. Medical issues might lower earning potential and result in high costs that strain investments and savings. Long-term financial risks can be decreased by maintaining healthy habits through a balanced diet, regular exercise, enough sleep, stress reduction, and preventative healthcare. Perfect health is unachievable, but regular attention to one's own well-being promotes longevity in the workplace, productivity, and the capacity to pursue financial objectives. Therefore, investing in one's health is a financial and personal obligation.

Another crucial method of asset protection is emergency savings. Throughout life, unforeseen circumstances like job loss, medical emergency, home repairs, car upkeep, or family obligations might arise. Without financial reserves, people could have to borrow money, sell investments, or liquidate important assets in adverse situations. An emergency fund serves as a safety net to cover unforeseen costs while preserving long-term investments and financial ambitions. While maintaining the financial advancement attained over years of steady work, this preparation lessens emotional decision-making.

Another crucial instrument for safeguarding priceless possessions is insurance. If left unprotected, dangers to homes, cars, businesses, health, and income could result in large financial losses. In exchange for steady monthly payments, appropriate insurance coverage shifts some financial risks to insurance companies. Insurance helps lessen the financial effects of unforeseen catastrophes, even though it cannot stop them from happening. The value of the assets being covered, family obligations, and individual circumstances must all be carefully considered when selecting the right coverage. By reducing the impact of significant unanticipated losses, effective insurance planning promotes long-term financial resilience.

Patience, self-control, and careful risk management are necessary for investment protection. Many investors ignore the significance of capital preservation in favor of concentrating only on increasing returns. Growth prospects and suitable risk levels must be balanced for investing to be successful. Diversification among many businesses, investment categories, and asset classes helps lower exposure to losses brought on by subpar performance in any one investment. Additionally, regular portfolio reviews guarantee that investing strategies stay in line with evolving personal circumstances and financial objectives. The goal of investment protection is to manage risk sensibly while keeping an eye on the big picture, not to eliminate it completely.

Another good strategy to safeguard important assets is to avoid taking on needless debt. Because debt payments lower available income for investing, saving, and handling unforeseen circumstances, excessive borrowing raises financial vulnerability. Unmanaged debt can seriously jeopardize houses, cars, businesses, or other valuable assets. Long-term wealth and financial flexibility are preserved by responsible borrowing, regular repayment, and careful financial planning. People who reduce needless debt are better able to safeguard the things they have put a lot of effort into acquiring.

In the current world, cybersecurity has grown in importance for safeguarding financial assets. Although they offer convenience, online banking, digital investments, electronic payments, and internet-based financial services also pose new threats. If the proper measures are not taken, identity theft, fraudulent transactions, phishing efforts, and cybercrime can cause large financial losses. These dangers can be decreased by using strong passwords, turning on extra security measures, routinely checking financial accounts, and exercising caution when disclosing personal information. Responsible asset management now requires the protection of digital financial data.

Asset protection is also aided by legal planning. In order to guarantee that valuable assets are managed in accordance with individual preferences, proper documentation, accurate financial records, updated beneficiary designations, wills, and other legal procedures are necessary. In addition to eliminating potential conflicts or needless financial issues, clear legal planning lowers uncertainty for family members. Periodically reviewing crucial legal documents enables modifications to account for evolving family situations, financial objectives, or legal needs. By assisting in the preservation of wealth for future generations, responsible planning extends financial safety beyond one's own lifetime.

Long-term financial success is also supported by the preservation of priceless tangible assets. Regular maintenance is necessary to maintain the operation and value of homes, cars, equipment, and commercial property. Delaying essential repairs frequently shortens the useful life of valuable assets and increases future costs. Rather than being a superfluous expense, routine maintenance is an investment in long-term preservation. Responsible maintenance of tangible assets lowers the risk of expensive emergencies while preserving their value.

Careful consideration should also be given to financial documents. Financial management is made easier while preventing misunderstandings and disagreements when bank accounts, investments, insurance policies, property ownership, tax records, and significant financial agreements are all properly documented. Maintaining accurate records enables people to track developments, spot anomalies, and react to crises or legal issues more skillfully. By giving a comprehensive picture of financial resources and liabilities, good record-keeping also facilitates well-informed decision-making.

Making deliberate lifestyle decisions is another way to safeguard important possessions. Regardless of income level, financial stability can be progressively weakened by going over budget, taking needless financial risks, or ignoring long-term planning. Reducing debt, building up financial reserves, and continuously saving money are all made possible by living within one's means. By lowering exposure to preventable financial troubles and promoting long-term wealth building, prudent everyday decisions offer ongoing safety.

In order to preserve key assets, family contact is crucial. Open communication among family members promotes mutual understanding on financial goals, duties, insurance coverage, legal planning, and long-term objectives. When couples collaborate on financial planning, they are frequently better equipped to safeguard home assets in unforeseen circumstances. By teaching the next generation the importance of careful planning, disciplined spending, and long-term thinking, teaching children healthy financial habits also increases future asset preservation.

Asset protection is further improved by ongoing financial education. Technology, banking rules, investment opportunities, and economic situations all change throughout time. People who are dedicated to learning become better at identifying dangers, assessing opportunities, and making wise decisions. Financial literacy boosts confidence while lowering susceptibility to fraud, bad investments, or expensive errors. Every facet of personal financial management is strengthened by lifelong learning, which turns into a continuous source of protection.

Frequent financial evaluations enable people to spot any flaws before they become serious issues. There are possibilities to make timely modifications by looking at financial goals, debt levels, insurance coverage, savings balances, investment performance, and budgets. Financial protection strategies may need to be updated in response to changing employment, growing families, buying property, or getting close to retirement. Frequent evaluations guarantee that priceless possessions are suitably safeguarded as life situations change.

In order to preserve riches, patience and discipline are still crucial. Emotional decisions made during times of excitement or uncertainty often lead to financial losses. Financial stability is frequently weakened by rashly selling investments, chasing unrealistic prospects, or ignoring long-term planning. People can safeguard assets while pursuing consistent growth by staying focused on well-thought-out methods. Maintaining current wealth is just as important to long-term success as generating new wealth.

In the end, securing precious assets is about preserving the outcomes of years of diligence, self-control, and careful financial decisions. Each asset is a chance to build future stability, adaptability, and independence. People build a solid foundation that supports long-term prosperity by safeguarding their earning potential, staying healthy, accumulating emergency savings, utilizing the right insurance, managing investments responsibly, cutting back on needless debt, securing financial information, keeping physical property, organizing financial records, and consistently expanding their financial knowledge. Wealth protection is motivated by wisdom rather than fear, understanding that financial success is enhanced when priceless assets are maintained with the same care and attention as they were created. People may make sure that their assets continue to support their families, help them achieve their goals, and provide opportunities for many years to come by making responsible everyday decisions and consistent planning.

Preparing For Challenges

Since no financial journey is entirely free from unforeseen barriers, preparing for adversities is a crucial component of creating long-lasting financial security. Everyone will probably run into circumstances that put their financial security to the test, regardless of their income level, profession, or stage of life. Economic downturns, unforeseen medical costs, job loss, family emergencies, growing living expenses, natural calamities, or changes in personal circumstances are a few examples of these difficulties. Even though nobody can pinpoint the precise moment when these things will happen, careful planning enables people to react with more resilience and confidence. A person's ability to handle money during prosperous times is simply one aspect of their financial success; another is how well they handle uncertain times without giving up on their long-term objectives.

Recognizing that uncertainty is a normal aspect of life is one of the most important lessons in preparing for challenges. Even the most well-organized people may run into unforeseen circumstances, despite the widespread belief that meticulous planning can solve every financial issue. Acknowledging this fact promotes preparation rather than dread. Financially responsible people set up processes that enable them to handle challenges with more assurance rather than hope that problems never occur. This way of thinking turns uncertainty from a cause of worry into an excuse for careful preparation and regular money management.

Keeping an emergency reserve is the first step towards building a solid financial foundation. People are often compelled to rely on debt when they have no savings, which makes unexpected needs daunting. Families may pay for essential requirements without interfering with long-term financial plans thanks to emergency reserves, which offer quick financial support during trying times. It takes time to build an emergency fund because each deposit increases financial stability as the fund grows gradually through monthly contributions. The mental strain that frequently accompanies unforeseen financial crises is lessened when emergency resources are known to be available.

Preparing for obstacles also heavily depends on responsible spending management. People who frequently spend more than they can afford frequently have little leeway when their income drops or their costs unexpectedly rise. Living within one's means allows one to modify expenditures during challenging times without having to deal with a financial catastrophe right away. Financial resilience is strengthened by careful budgeting, deliberate shopping, and avoiding needless debt since these actions protect resources that could be crucial in an emergency. Long before problems arise, stability is established by responsible spending practices.

Another crucial step in getting ready for financial volatility is cutting back on needless debt. Excessive debt reduces flexibility during times of lower income and raises monthly financial commitments. Resources that may be used to support necessities or bolster savings are consumed by interest payments. People might strengthen their resilience to unforeseen financial losses by lowering debt gradually and borrowing sensibly. Because fewer financial obligations need to be addressed right away during difficult times, lower debt levels lead to more freedom.

Additionally, diversifying sources of income improves financial readiness. Relying solely on one source of income can make you more vulnerable to unforeseen job changes or adverse economic conditions. More financial flexibility can be achieved by creating other revenue streams through consulting, freelancing, part-time jobs, investments, or entrepreneurial endeavors. Several sources of income provide more chances for long-term financial success while lowering reliance on any one source. During trying times, even a small additional source of income can be quite helpful.

Another effective strategy to get ready for upcoming issues is career growth. People who consistently enhance their abilities, broaden their knowledge, and maintain flexibility in response to shifting workplace demands are better able to hold onto their jobs and take advantage of new opportunities. During economic downturns, professional development lowers the likelihood of long-term unemployment while increasing earning potential. Because people may adapt to new industries, technology, and professional duties as circumstances change, lifelong learning fosters resilience.

Financial readiness is also greatly aided by insurance. Without sufficient protection, medical emergencies, accidents, disabilities, property damage, or unplanned income loss can result in extreme costs. Appropriate insurance coverage protects long-term financial advancement while lessening the financial impact of these occurrences, enabling people to recoup more successfully. Instead of being seen as a needless expense, insurance should be seen as a useful instrument for controlling substantial risks. Insurance strengthens the financial safety net and promotes greater stability during unpredictable times when combined with emergency savings.

Building emotional resilience is another aspect of preparing for obstacles. Decision-making can be impacted by the stress, anxiety, frustration, and uncertainty that financial troubles frequently cause. Emotional responses can cause people to make rash decisions like taking out unneeded loans, selling investments too soon, or giving up on long-term financial ambitions. Developing self-control, patience, and deliberate decision-making enables people to react composedly even in trying situations. During unpredictable times, emotional resilience promotes sound judgment and helps maintain financial stability.

Another beneficial practice is to plan ahead for anticipated future expenses. Many financial problems are caused by neglecting to budget for normal spending rather than by genuinely unexpected events. Expenses for home upkeep, auto repairs, schooling, holidays, insurance renewals, and medical care frequently occur on set timetables. By setting aside modest sums of money each month for these future commitments, you can spread out the financial load over time and lessen the chance of experiencing financial strain when these costs ultimately arise.

A key component of successful financial planning is flexibility. Marriage, having children, changing careers, moving, retiring, or experiencing health issues all alter one's life circumstances. While keeping an eye on long-term objectives, financial planning should adjust to these shifting circumstances. People who routinely evaluate and modify their investments, insurance policies, savings programs, and budgets are better equipped to handle unforeseen events. Without sacrificing fundamental financial concepts, flexibility enables financial strategies to continue being useful and efficient.

Families that communicate well are better equipped to handle obstacles in the future. Cooperation and mutual understanding are fostered by candid conversations regarding financial objectives, obligations, emergency preparations, and spending priorities. Family members who are familiar with home finances are better able to cooperate in trying times. When unforeseen circumstances arise, open communication minimizes miscommunication and enables everyone to participate in preserving financial stability.

Keeping reasonable expectations is another way to prepare for obstacles. The path to financial success is rarely entirely straightforward. Long-term financial growth often involves periods of slower progress, unforeseen costs, and temporary setbacks. People who are aware of this fact do not give up when things get tough. They see setbacks as transient challenges that can be surmounted with perseverance, self-control, and careful preparation rather than as failures. During difficult times, this viewpoint boosts confidence and promotes perseverance.

Frequent financial assessments facilitate efficient planning by spotting possible flaws before they become significant issues. Instead of waiting for disasters to arise, people can make proactive modifications by reviewing their spending patterns, savings efforts, debt levels, insurance coverage, investment performance, and financial goals. These evaluations promote ongoing development while reiterating sound financial practices that bolster long-term resilience.

Developing solid interpersonal ties also helps with financial readiness. During trying circumstances, supportive family members, dependable friends, mentors, and professional advisers offer important motivation, useful guidance, and emotional support. Strong relationships provide additional resources that help people overcome obstacles more skillfully, even though financial independence is still a crucial aim. Working together and pooling knowledge frequently results in better solutions than trying to solve every issue on your own.

Keeping a realistic yet optimistic attitude is another important part of preparedness. While realism promotes sensible preparation, optimism fosters motivation and hope. Combining these mindsets enables people to acknowledge that obstacles necessitate careful planning while yet having faith in future success. This well-rounded viewpoint helps people make better financial judgments in the face of shifting conditions by preventing both needless anxiety and irrational overconfidence.

The confidence that comes with preparing for challenges is probably the biggest advantage. People who have emergency funds, carefully manage their debt, acquire useful skills, keep the right insurance, and routinely check their financial plans are more at ease when faced with uncertainty. They have made significant efforts to improve their capacity to react appropriately, even though they are aware that they cannot control every situation. Even in uncertain times, this confidence promotes ongoing progress and lessens financial stress.

Building financial resilience through regular routines, careful planning, and prudent decision-making is ultimately the key to being ready for challenges. Every constructive activity, whether it be consistent saving, debt reduction, career skill development, insurance maintenance, or developing financial awareness, contributes to increased preparedness for whatever the future may hold. Although obstacles are unavoidable in life, they don't have to stand in the way of long-term financial success. Through perseverance, self-control, adaptability, ongoing education, and meticulous planning, people build a solid financial foundation that can endure unforeseen challenges while still advancing toward worthwhile objectives. This dedication to preparedness eventually turns uncertainty into opportunity, proving that long-term financial security is created by acquiring the skills, information, and self-assurance required to conquer obstacles with discernment and fortitude rather than by avoiding them.

Building A Strong Foundation

The capacity to work, save, invest, and accumulate wealth is not the only indicator of long-term financial success. The capacity to safeguard what has already been constructed serves as an equal yardstick. Protection is a crucial component of healthy money management since every financial decision involves a time, effort, and sacrifice commitment. This chapter is important because it serves as a reminder that long-term success requires both the creation of resources and their protection from preventable threats. When growth and protection cooperate, financial security is at its highest. Unnecessary vulnerability results from one without the other. Even though someone has accumulated valuable assets over many years, if proper preparation has not been done, one unforeseen disaster might undermine that progress. Therefore, deliberate planning that protects both current accomplishments and future opportunities is necessary to build a secure future.

By putting the concepts discussed in this chapter into practice, people's perspectives on financial responsibility are altered. Rather than presuming that challenging circumstances won't arise, they start making sensible preparations for potential outcomes that are a part of daily life. Unexpected illness, property damage, accidents, natural disasters, economic instability, or job changes become manageable difficulties instead of crises that totally upend financial stability. People who are prepared feel more confident because they know they have put in place workable mechanisms to lessen the financial effect of life's uncertainties. Because vital resources are safeguarded, families feel more at ease. Because financial plans are made to support long-term objectives even in the face of unforeseen circumstances, they become more resilient. This proactive approach lessens anxiety about the future while promoting careful decision-making.

Regardless of income or gained wealth, disregarding these principles might have detrimental effects. Many people pay little attention to safeguarding their financial resources and instead concentrate solely on developing them. Consequently, situations that could have been handled more skillfully with proper planning could undermine years of focused labor. Savings meant for future objectives may be depleted by emergency costs. Costly repairs for valuable property may put a strain on one's capacity to make ends meet. Families can suffer needlessly as a result of crucial financial safeguards being disregarded. Even those with substantial assets may find that they are vulnerable in uncertain times due to poor preparedness. Lack of protection frequently turns controllable circumstances into persistent financial difficulties. While not all challenges can be avoided, preparation greatly lessens their long-term effects.

Responsible financial protection has far-reaching effects in real life that go well beyond saving money. People feel more emotionally secure because they are more equipped to deal with unforeseen situations. Because financial planning takes into account both regular obligations and unforeseen circumstances, families enjoy increased stability. Knowing that they have made significant efforts to help their loved ones through trying times gives parents a sense of confidence. Because they recognize the value of safeguarding the resources that sustain their way of life, business owners become more resilient. Unexpected failures are less likely to impede long-term progress, which strengthens retirement planning. Above all, financial security frees people from continually worrying about what might happen in the future, allowing them to concentrate on development, opportunity, and meaningful life.

By the end of this chapter, you will be able to recognize financial risks that could jeopardize your long-term stability and devise workable solutions to lessen their effects, develop a well-rounded financial protection plan that supports both current obligations and long-term objectives, and bolster your financial confidence by fusing careful planning with regular long-term planning.

Take Caroline as an example; she diligently managed household spending while saving for many years. She thought that conserving money was enough to secure one's financial future. She had never examined her financial protection plans, so when a significant storm damaged a portion of her house, she found that numerous crucial repairs were not sufficiently covered. She used a large portion of her meticulously saved money to pay for unforeseen expenses. Despite being challenging, the experience inspired her to enhance all facets of her financial preparation. She increased her emergency fund, examined her insurance coverage, arranged crucial financial records, and developed a strategy to safeguard her expanding investments. A few years later, another unforeseen incident happened, but this time she handled it coolly since preparation had taken the place of uncertainty. Caroline came to see that safeguarding financial advancement is as crucial as generating it.

This idea is demonstrated by a short narrative. On nearby hillsides, two families constructed houses. The first family paid little care to maintaining the roof and fortifying the walls in favor of almost totally adorning the interior with lovely furnishings and decorations. The second family built a cozy house as well, but they did routine roof inspections, fixed minor issues before they got worse, and strengthened the building as needed. Both houses experienced the same weather when a strong storm finally arrived. One was severely harmed because minor flaws had gone unnoticed. Because meticulous preparation had been finished far in advance of the storm, the other stayed sturdy. The similar pattern applies to financial safety. When difficulties eventually arise, preparation made during peaceful times gives you strength.

The foundation of a towering building serves as a helpful metaphor for financial safety. People frequently marvel at a building's striking height without ever being able to see the foundation that lies beneath it. However, that invisible structure is the foundation of every story. The building's ability to endure weather changes, heavy use, and the passage of time is positively correlated with the strength of the foundation. The goal of financial protection is the same. The visible structure is represented by savings, investments, businesses, and valuable assets; the secret foundation that supports everything above it is formed by careful preparation. Even remarkable financial success is susceptible in the absence of that base. Because stability has been purposefully built, progress can proceed with more assurance.

Use the Protect Preserve Prosper Framework to start putting these concepts into practice right away. Start by determining which financial resources—savings, investments, property, income, business interests, and family obligations—are most crucial to your long-term well-being. Next, assess the hazards that might have an impact on each of these categories. Take into account unforeseen costs, health issues, property damage, legal obligations, or job changes. Once these risks have been identified, evaluate the workable safeguards that are currently in place and identify any areas that might require improvement. Boost emergency funds, keep up-to-date insurance, arrange crucial financial records, and establish precise plans for handling unforeseen circumstances. Make sure your protection plans continue to reflect your evolving financial situation and personal objectives by scheduling routine yearly evaluations. To make financial protection a habit rather than a one-time activity, repeat this practice frequently.

This framework's efficacy stems from its ability to strike a balance between planning and adaptability. Fear or undue caution should never be the driving forces behind financial protection. Rather, it should give assurance by guaranteeing that appropriate safeguards are in place while permitting ongoing financial expansion. Over the course of a lifetime, circumstances naturally change. Families grow, businesses grow, income rises, and responsibilities change. Frequent assessment enables protective strategies to adjust as conditions change without necessitating total reconstruction.

Realizing that prevention is frequently considerably less expensive than recovery is another important lesson. Oftentimes, small efforts today eliminate much bigger problems later. Compared to the work needed to recover from avoidable financial failures, reviewing crucial documents, keeping emergency reserves, updating financial records, comprehending insurance coverage, and getting ready for potential hazards take comparatively little time. As a result, careful planning turns into an investment that safeguards years of diligence and sound financial practices.

Remembering that financial security fosters confidence rather than restricting potential is equally crucial. Some people erroneously think that being ready for possible hazards is a sign of pessimism. In actuality, careful planning decreases uncertainty, which leads to more freedom. Knowing that they have put in place workable safeguards gives people more confidence to pursue investments, job prospects, business ideas, and personal objectives because they know that unforeseen challenges are less likely to impede long-term success.

Future generations are also strengthened by robust financial protection. When financial obligations are well-organized and vital resources are appropriately safeguarded, families gain. Through common examples, children learn responsibility and long-term thinking through careful planning. Because crucial choices have been made before situations need quick action, loved ones feel more secure. As a result, protection becomes both a component of financial planning and an expression of concern.

Consider whether your present financial strategy safeguards the advancements you have already made. Which aspect of your financial life might gain the most from better planning right now? If you knew that your family and significant financial assets were better safeguarded from unforeseen difficulties, how would that affect your confidence? What doable steps may you take this week to improve your long-term financial stability? How can you develop a long-term practice of conducting regular financial evaluations that will safeguard your future for many years to come?

Every significant financial accomplishment should be carefully safeguarded. Careful planning and preparation increase the value of the work put into earning, saving, investing, and accumulating wealth. Treating protection as a necessary partner to financial progress rather than an afterthought can help you continue to fortify your future. Every sensible choice you make, every routine assessment, and every useful precaution you take gives the life you are building an additional degree of solidity. When planning becomes a regular practice backed by perseverance, accountability, and a clear goal, long-term financial confidence increases. You will continue to create possibilities for long-term success while constructing a future that is not only prosperous but also sturdy, secure, and equipped to endure the unexpected.

CHAPTER X

Lifetime Wealth Legacy

Family Financial Planning

One of the most important parts of creating long-term wealth is family financial planning since financial success is even more significant when it supports loved ones' security, well-being, and future prospects. Although individual financial accountability is crucial, careful family planning produces stability that spans generations. Every financial choice made in a household has the ability to affect not just the living conditions of the present but also future prospects for education, career choices, retirement, health, and the financial habits that children will inherit. As family members collaborate to achieve shared objectives, a well-structured financial plan gives them direction, improves relationships, and fosters a sense of purpose.

Open and honest communication is the cornerstone of a successful family financial plan. Although money is generally seen as a delicate subject, avoiding financial discussions often results in miscommunication, irrational expectations, and needless strife. In a respectful and cooperative environment, families can address income, expenses, savings objectives, debt obligations, and future aspirations. In addition to fostering shared accountability for accomplishing long-term goals, open communication enables each family member to comprehend the financial status of the household. Everyone gets more invested in the family's future prosperity, and trust increases when financial decisions are made collaboratively rather than separately.

Establishing common financial objectives gives family planning direction. Financial decisions are influenced by the distinct values, priorities, and aspirations of each household. While some families emphasize education, travel, business ownership, retirement planning, charitable giving, or building financial stability for future generations, others may concentrate on buying a home. It is easier to make sure that everyday financial decisions support long-term goals rather than fleeting impulses when these shared goals are clearly defined. Goals also provide family members a sense of purpose for their financial discipline and sacrifices, which helps them stay motivated during difficult times.

A crucial component of family financial planning is developing a workable home budget. A budget makes it possible to carefully distribute income among necessities, savings, debt repayment, investments, and leisure activities. By guaranteeing that financial resources are used purposefully, a realistic budget fosters confidence rather than restricting freedom. Regular budget reviews help families become more conscious of their spending patterns and find ways to increase their financial efficiency. By giving each dollar a purpose, this strategy promotes accountability and lowers uncertainty.

Financial stability and family cohesion are strengthened when people save together. Setting monthly savings targets for retirement, significant purchases, crises, education, or vacations fosters a sense of collaboration as family members work together to achieve shared goals. The importance of perseverance and self-control is demonstrated by even modest savings that are steadily collected over time. Youngsters who witness their parents consistently saving money tend to adopt better financial practices as well, realizing that long-term planning yields significant benefits. Because it teaches responsibility, postponing gratification, and the value of future planning, saving becomes more than just a financial activity.

A key component of family financial planning is emergency readiness. Household finances might be severely strained by unforeseen circumstances like medical difficulties, job loss, home maintenance, natural disasters, or family obligations. By enabling these circumstances to be handled without significantly depending on debt or interfering with long-term financial objectives, an emergency fund offers important safety. Families can respond calmly and confidently in trying situations when they know that financial reserves are available. When unforeseen difficulties emerge, preparation lowers stress and increases resilience.

A better financial future for the whole family is another benefit of responsible debt management. Because a large amount of household income must be used for repayment rather than savings or investments, excessive debt limits financial flexibility. Families that put a high priority on cutting back on needless debt have more chances to accumulate wealth and experience less financial strain.

Before making significant financial commitments, it is important to have an honest conversation about borrowing choices to make sure that debt is used to support long-term objectives rather than transient desires. Effective debt management increases prospects for financial growth while safeguarding future earnings.

Another crucial aspect of family financial planning is education. By enhancing financial literacy, employment prospects, and decision-making skills, education investments benefit both parents and kids. Children are better prepared for greater financial independence in the future when their parents teach them about budgeting, saving, investing, and appropriate spending. Because financial behaviors formed throughout childhood often persist into adulthood, these teachings frequently have long-lasting benefits. Future generations are better prepared to steer clear of typical financial blunders and accumulate long-term wealth when curiosity about money management is fostered.

Another crucial component of safeguarding family income is insurance. The financial impact of unforeseen circumstances that might otherwise jeopardize household stability is lessened by health insurance, life insurance, disability coverage, property insurance, and other types of protection. Even though insurance has recurring expenses, it offers important stability by assisting families in recovering from unanticipated events without depleting savings or accruing excessive debt. Appropriate coverage ensures that important financial resources are safeguarded when they are most required, reflecting careful forethought rather than fear.

Because it lessens the possibility of future financial reliance on children or other family members, retirement planning is a crucial part of family financial planning. People who consistently save for retirement are able to preserve their financial resources for future generations while maintaining a higher level of freedom. Retirement planning gives families more flexibility and dignity in later life, which is why they incorporate it into their entire financial strategy. Long-term retirement planning also makes it possible to spend more time with loved ones and have more meaningful experiences without having to worry about money.

Making careful decisions is necessary to strike a balance between current demands and long-term objectives. Families naturally desire to give each other fun events, chances, and celebrations. However, continuously putting short-term gratification ahead of long-term security frequently results in long-term financial problems. In order to achieve balance, successful family financial planning continually invests in long-term stability while leaving space for enjoyment. Without compromising one for the other, this well-rounded strategy enables family members to value both present experiences and upcoming potential.

The financial success of a family is also influenced by career planning. Promoting lifelong learning, skill development, and professional growth raises earning potential and promotes financial flexibility. Supporting one another's academic and professional aspirations benefits families since increased earning potential leads to more stable households. When professional growth is paired with sound financial practices, more resources are produced that support investments, savings, and future prospects.

Families can stay in line with evolving conditions by doing regular financial evaluations. As children grow, occupations shift, money varies, or retirement draws near, household requirements inevitably vary. It is possible to make deliberate changes while preserving long-term direction by reviewing budgets, savings objectives, investments, insurance coverage, and financial priorities. These frequent conversations promote flexibility and stop minor financial issues from growing into more serious ones over time. Flexibility guarantees that financial plans stay focused on future goals while continuing to meet the family's present needs.

One of the best things parents can do for their children is to teach them financial responsibility. Children learn the value of money beyond mere consumption when they are included in age-appropriate conversations about budgeting, saving, charitable giving, and responsible spending. Giving kids the opportunity to handle tiny sums of money teaches them patience, accountability, and decision-making in useful ways. These early encounters foster habits that lead to lifetime financial success while boosting self-confidence.

By refocusing attention from continual consumption to appreciation of available resources and opportunities, gratitude also improves family financial planning. Gratitude-practicing families are frequently less impacted by social comparison or needless expenditure motivated by looks. In addition to promoting deliberate financial decisions that support important priorities rather than fleeting pleasures, appreciating what has already been accomplished increases contentment. Healthy connections with money and one another are fostered by gratitude.

The advantages of family planning are extended beyond the current generation by creating a financial legacy. Inherited wealth is only one aspect of a legacy. It also encompasses knowledge, discipline, charity, ideals, habits, and responsible decision-making. Families that regularly manage their finances well provide an example for future generations, encouraging them to build on a solid financial basis. Since knowledge makes it possible to develop, safeguard, and maintain future wealth, passing on strong financial principles frequently proves to be even more beneficial than passing on actual assets.

In the end, family financial planning is about making deliberate everyday choices that will lead to a stable, secure, and fulfilling future. In order to create a cohesive strategy that benefits all members of the household, it integrates communication, shared goals, disciplined saving, responsible spending, debt management, education, protection, and long-term planning. When financial success improves relationships, lowers needless stress, increases opportunities, and gives loved ones long-term security, it becomes more fulfilling. Families build financial foundations that can sustain not only their current needs but also the aspirations of future generations through persistent cooperation, tolerance, adaptability, and dedication to common ideals. Every prudent choice taken collectively becomes an investment in a future characterized by opportunity, stability, resiliency, and long-term prosperity.

Creating Lasting Impact

Since true wealth goes well beyond material achievement or personal comfort, making a lasting influence is one of the most significant results of leading a healthy financial life. When financial success enhances family well-being, builds communities, opens doors for future generations, and reflects personal ideals, it becomes more important. While achieving financial security is a crucial objective, the best indicator of success is frequently how well financial resources, expertise, and experiences are applied to enhance the lives of others. Consistent decisions that strike a balance between individual prosperity, accountability, generosity, and long-term vision have lasting effects.

Realizing that financial success entails both opportunity and responsibility is one of the first steps in making a lasting effect. Money is not the ultimate goal or a gauge of one's own value. Rather, it functions as a tool that can support significant objectives, foster personal development, offer security, and promote constructive change. People who comprehend this viewpoint concentrate on making smart use of their financial resources in addition to accumulating them. Every financial choice becomes a chance to express one's ideals and have a significant impact on the future.

Building a solid financial foundation is the first step towards making a lasting influence. People who regularly engage in responsible budgeting, mindful spending, regular saving, prudent investing, and meticulous planning establish stability that enables them to look past their current financial worries. Freedom to make decisions based on long-term priorities rather than ongoing financial pressure is provided by financial security. Without sacrificing one's own financial well-being, this stability makes it possible to support loved ones, give to worthy organizations, seek fulfilling employment, and invest in future generations.

Influence on family members is one of the most important ways people make a lasting difference. Observing parents, grandparents, family members, and reliable role models is a common way to pick up financial habits. Children are more likely to adopt similar behaviors throughout their own lives if they observe good money management, disciplined saving, mindful spending, and generous giving. Financial decisions made on a daily basis become significant lessons that influence attitudes toward money in the future. The advantages of teaching family members about long-term planning, saving, budgeting, and financial responsibility go well beyond one generation.

Setting a good example has a greater impact than just giving advise. Friends and family often see how people react to chances, financial difficulties, and daily choices. Being patient, disciplined, honest, and well-prepared inspires others to follow suit. People are frequently motivated by persistent efforts to make responsible decisions even in trying situations rather than by flawless financial accomplishment. The influence of financial advice and encouragement is strengthened by personal example, which establishes credibility.

In order to make a lasting impression, education is also crucial. By imparting financial knowledge to others, people might steer clear of typical blunders and get more self-assurance in handling their finances. Discussions about budgeting, debt management, investing, saving, and financial planning promote well-informed decision-making that is advantageous to both families and communities. Professional knowledge is not necessary for financial education. Others looking for more financial stability can benefit much from everyday experiences, lessons acquired from setbacks, and useful routines.

Another effective strategy for making a lasting impression is generosity. When financial success offers chances to assist others, it takes on greater significance. Supporting charitable organizations, helping family members through trying times, funding educational opportunities, volunteering, or taking part in community projects are all examples of acts of generosity. A mindset of abundance rather than scarcity is reflected in generosity. By enhancing the lives of people and fortifying communities, it shows that financial resources may be used for goals other than self-interest. Even small deeds of generosity have beneficial ramifications that frequently go well beyond their immediate worth.

Supporting future generations via careful planning is another way to make a lasting effect. Long-term family stability is influenced by retirement planning, setting aside money for education, keeping the right insurance, preserving crucial financial records, and creating estate plans. In addition to helping to protect financial resources that might continue to assist future generations, proper planning lowers uncertainty for loved ones. Making plans for tomorrow's needs now shows concern, accountability, and dedication to the welfare of the family.

Maintaining personal values while achieving financial success is another crucial component of long-lasting influence. Integrity should be strengthened rather than weakened by wealth. Respect for others, ethical decision-making, honest business methods, and responsible stewardship all foster trust that endures far longer than monetary gains alone. People who uphold moral principles while accumulating wealth frequently gain enduring esteem since their achievements demonstrate both their character and their financial prowess. Integrity leaves a legacy that goes beyond monetary gains.

Long-lasting influence is also influenced by ongoing personal development. People who are dedicated to lifelong learning, professional skill development, leadership, and knowledge expansion are better equipped to make significant contributions. Career prospects are strengthened by personal development, which also improves one's capacity to mentor others, resolve issues, and offer insightful advice. The information acquired by lifelong learning turns into a tool that helps everyone who gains knowledge from their experience, not just the individual.

Another significant source of long-lasting influence is the development of solid relationships. When financial achievement is shared with dependable friends, family, coworkers, and community partners, it takes on greater significance. Cooperation, mutual growth, emotional support, and shared learning are all promoted by healthy relationships. Because deep connections enhance both individual contentment and group achievement, investing time in relationships frequently yields benefits that far outweigh financial returns. Opportunities to influence others through support, mentoring, and shared experiences are also created by positive interactions.

When financial choices support companies and organizations that add value to society, responsible investing can also have a long-lasting effect. Investing in successful businesses promotes community development, economic growth, employment, and innovation. People who are aware of the wider impact of their financial decisions understand that investments can support both beneficial economic development and personal riches. This viewpoint promotes careful consideration of how financial resources impact individual objectives as well as larger societies.

The idea of making a lasting impact is also reflected in environmental responsibility. The responsible management of shared resources is facilitated by thoughtful consumption, cutting back on waste, encouraging sustainable behaviors, and making well-informed purchasing decisions. Everyday spending decisions have the potential to promote a healthy future since financial decisions frequently have an impact on environmental results. In addition to creating financial security, responsible stewardship acknowledges that long-term success involves protecting resources for future generations.

Since genuine influence takes years to establish, it takes patience to create enduring impact. Consistently practicing daily routines gradually shapes one's character, connections with others, and financial results. Over time, modest deeds of kindness, responsibility, education, and careful planning add up to substantial contributions. Because consistent behavior fosters respect, trust, and long-lasting change, people who stick to good habits frequently have an impact that goes well beyond their initial expectations.

Additionally, humility enhances long-lasting effects. Instead of encouraging conceit, financial success can promote thankfulness. While keeping perspective, acknowledging the contributions of mentors, family, coworkers, and opportunities fosters appreciation. Humble people cherish other people's contributions, stay receptive to new ideas, and use their accomplishments to uplift rather than depress those around them. This mindset strengthens bonds and has a favorable impact on one's personal and professional life.

Another trait that helps create a meaningful legacy is resilience. Every financial journey has obstacles, disappointments, and unforeseen problems. People who handle these situations with tenacity, tolerance, and moral rectitude teach others important lessons. Their example shows that conquering obstacles with sensible choices and persistent effort is what defines long-term success rather than avoiding suffering. Future generations are frequently greatly inspired by these experiences.

Realizing that wealth serves its greatest purpose when it promotes something bigger than individual success is perhaps the most important part of making a lasting influence. Opportunities to build stronger families, educate the next generation, give back to the community, promote responsible leadership, and support worthwhile causes are all made possible by financial security. Because good habits become traditions, lessons become wisdom, and generosity provides possibilities that span generations, the impact of careful financial decisions frequently lasts long after specific transactions are forgotten.

Using financial success to leave the world in a better state than when you found it is ultimately the key to making a lasting effect. Every wise choice, every lesson imparted, every opportunity generated, and every act of kindness adds to a legacy that goes beyond individual financial achievements. People create lives that inspire self-assurance, accountability, and hope through disciplined money management, ongoing education, moral behavior, careful preparation, solid relationships, and a dedication to assisting others. These persistent efforts have a long-lasting positive impact on families, communities, and future generations. True financial success is determined not just by the amount of money amassed over a lifetime but also by the beneficial impact that character, wealth, and wisdom continue to have long after the financial objectives themselves have been met.

Maintaining Wealth Habits

Building wealth is just the start of the trip; thus, maintaining wealthy habits is one of the most crucial tasks in attaining long-term financial success. Long after significant milestones have been attained, the behaviors that lead to financial stability must persist. Many people put a lot of effort into increasing their income, paying off debt, or expanding their investments, but long-term success depends on continuing to engage in the habits that made those accomplishments possible. Temporary discipline or sporadic effort does not sustain financial success. It is maintained by daily decisions that show accountability, tolerance, and dedication to long-term objectives. People who maintain sound financial practices are better equipped to protect their wealth as their circumstances change over time.

The cornerstone of sustaining wealthy habits is consistency. Daily small financial decisions frequently have a bigger impact than sporadic big ones. Stability is created over time by continuing to save on a regular basis, making judicious purchases, monitoring financial progress, and making steady investments. These behaviors may seem commonplace, but when they are sustained over a long period of time, their cumulative impact becomes astonishing because responsible behavior becomes ingrained in daily life rather than being sporadic endeavors driven by short-term objectives; wealth increases and stays stable.

Avoiding complacency is one of the biggest obstacles after making financial progress. A false sense of security can arise from reaching significant milestones like paying off debt, accumulating funds, buying a house, or boosting investments. Some people start letting go of the habits that made them successful because they think they don't need strict spending guidelines or meticulous budgeting. However, unforeseen changes in the economy, medical problems, work changes, or family obligations can all affect one's financial situation. Long-term financial stability is maintained while ongoing protection against these uncertainties is provided by upholding sound financial practices.

Regardless of economic level, living below one's means is still a crucial practice. It is normal to enjoy certain lifestyle enhancements as earnings rise, but permitting spending to expand at the same rate as income frequently restricts future financial progress. When extra money is spent right away on bigger purchases rather than being put toward savings, investments, or future prospects, lifestyle inflation takes place. Long after others have reached a financial plateau, those who continue to accumulate wealth while maintaining modest spending habits have more financial flexibility.

Even after major financial objectives have been met, regular saving should continue. Savings build resilience in the face of unforeseen difficulties, support future opportunities, and offer stability. Regular contributions boost financial confidence and reinforce disciplined money management, whether the goal is retirement, school, travel, business prospects, or future family requirements. Saving becomes less about responding to short-term objectives and more about preserving a solid financial base that can accommodate shifting priorities over the course of a lifetime.

Another habit that helps create long-term wealth is regular investing. Emotional responses are one of the biggest threats to long-term success because financial markets inherently go through cycles of boom and fall. Long-term outcomes are frequently better for those who continue to invest in accordance with well-considered plans rather than fleeting market conditions. Investments can develop slowly over many years if patience is maintained and impetuous judgments are avoided during uncertain times.

Regardless of expertise, financial education should continue to be a habit. Throughout life, financial regulations, technology, investment opportunities, and economic conditions all change. Maintaining a commitment to learning helps people make better judgments and adjust to changing conditions. Stronger financial confidence can be attained through reading financial resources, learning about personal finance, honing professional abilities, and gaining real-world experience. Lifelong learning guarantees that when financial resources increase, so does financial knowledge.

By giving people the chance to assess their success and make deliberate changes, regular financial assessments support the maintenance of sound wealth habits. People can identify their strengths and opportunities for growth by reviewing their financial goals, savings, investments, insurance coverage, and budgets. These evaluations should be seen as regular procedures that promote ongoing achievement rather than as indicators of financial difficulties. Consistent financial health monitoring keeps long-term objectives in focus while preventing minor problems from growing into bigger ones.

Maintaining wealthy habits also heavily relies on gratitude. People who value their financial advancement are frequently less swayed by pointless comparisons or temptation to overspend. Gratitude permits ongoing development while promoting contentment. Grateful people concentrate on using money to achieve important objectives, build relationships, and enhance their quality of life rather than chasing wealth only for appearances or social acclaim. This viewpoint lessens needless financial strain while promoting more prudent spending choices.

Because generosity serves as a reminder that financial achievement presents chances to favorably impact the lives of others, it further promotes healthy wealth practices. A healthy relationship with money is created by sharing resources responsibly through charitable giving, community support, or lending a hand to loved ones when necessary. Generosity reinforces the idea that financial achievement can have advantages beyond self-interest and promotes careful stewardship as opposed to an overwhelming commitment to material prosperity.

In the end, sustaining wealthy habits calls for constant dedication as opposed to fleeting inspiration. Consistent saving, prudent spending, disciplined investing, ongoing education, frequent financial evaluations, thankfulness, giving, and careful planning all contribute to financial success. These behaviors encourage ongoing development and long-term financial security while offering stability in the face of shifting conditions. Long-lasting wealth is the result of numerous wise decisions made repeatedly over time rather than a single exceptional one. People who stick to these values build financial lives that are characterized by self-assurance, resiliency, independence, and the capacity to pursue worthwhile objectives for both themselves and future generations.

The Journey Continues

Every significant financial accomplishment eventually poses a crucial query. After the objectives are achieved and the years of work are over, what long-term effects will be left? When financial success transcends personal comfort and generates opportunity, security, wisdom, and support for others, it achieves its ultimate goal. Wealth is determined not just by accumulation but also by the responsible management, protection, sharing, and transfer of wealth through deliberate choices. This chapter is important because it focuses on making a lasting impact that will continue to help future generations rather than just accumulating financial resources. Making wise financial decisions throughout one's life is made much more useful when those decisions encourage others to lead responsible, giving, disciplined, and purposeful lives. Leaving behind belongings alone is not the best way to leave a financial legacy. Long after individual accomplishments are finished, it is leaving behind chances, preparedness, and principles that continue to provide great outcomes.

By putting the concepts discussed in this chapter into practice, people's perceptions of success are altered. They start thinking about the long-term impact of every financial action rather than only concentrating on immediate successes or personal benefit. Because it promotes future family security, saving takes on greater significance. Because investing creates opportunities that can go beyond one's own lifetime, it becomes more meaningful. Planning responsibly becomes more than just an organizational exercise; it becomes an act of care for loved ones. People start teaching sound financial practices by setting a consistent example and using both terminology. When practical financial decisions are discussed alongside ideals, family interactions become more deliberate. Because resources are carefully controlled before being donated, generosity becomes more considerate. This more comprehensive view turns wealth into a tool for fostering relationships, promoting accountability, and generating opportunities that keep expanding over time.

If these guidelines are disregarded, years of diligent work may have significantly less of an impact than anticipated. When money is amassed without careful preparation, it can lead to misunderstandings, arguments, or needless worry for family members. Due to the constant postponement of discussions about money, responsibility, and long-term planning, important values might never be shared. Financial assets may be passed down to families without the knowledge necessary to manage them properly. Opportunities to prepare, educate, and mentor future generations may subtly vanish if attention is solely focused on the current situation. Even substantial financial success can lose a lot of its long-term worth without deliberate planning. A legacy doesn't just happen. Consistent behavior, careful planning, and deliberate choices made repeatedly throughout life are what make it.

Building a meaningful financial legacy has far-reaching effects in real life that go far beyond financial records or tangible belongings. Because significant obligations have been properly planned and communicated, families feel more confident. Children pick up discipline by seeing decent financial practices that are consistently displayed over a long period of time. When financially responsible people voluntarily donate their time, expertise, support, and resources, communities gain. Because careful planning equips future leaders for sustained success, businesses grow stronger. People feel more at rest since they are aware that they have taken significant action to lessen uncertainty for the people they love the most. People who may never completely understand how much their possibilities were affected by the deliberate choices made long before they came are frequently impacted by prudent financial stewardship.

By the end of this chapter, you will be able to organize your financial decisions in a way that strengthens family stability, preserves significant opportunities, and leaves a lasting positive impact beyond your own lifetime. You will also be able to develop habits that encourage future generations to manage financial resources responsibly by setting a consistent example.

Take Robert as an example, who carefully managed his finances while building a successful career over several decades. As retirement drew near, he came to the conclusion that amassing wealth by itself would not provide a significant legacy. He started putting critical financial paperwork in order, issuing clear instructions for his family, talking to his kids about financial principles, and teaching them the significance of saving, investing, giving, and making wise decisions. He engaged them in discussions about planning, budgeting, charitable giving, and long-term thinking rather than just offering cash assistance. Years later, his children frequently stated that the confidence, wisdom, and self-control they acquired from his example were the best gifts they got rather than the money they inherited. Robert saw that genuine prosperity encompassed both material possessions and the discernment required to manage them sensibly.

This fact is demonstrated via a brief narrative. For many years, an elderly craftsman created exquisite furniture that was adored by everyone in his neighborhood. Rather than finishing every task by himself, he brought his student into the workshop every day as retirement drew near. He gently described why specific materials were chosen, how meticulous measurements avoided future issues, and why speed should never come at the expense of quality. Because the knowledge underlying the artistry had been purposefully transmitted, his pupil continued to produce outstanding work even after the craftsman eventually retired. The expertise, discipline, and spirit that had been passed down to a new generation were the permanent legacy, even though the furniture was still valued. The same idea applies to financial wisdom. Even though resources may eventually be spent, the values and practices that go along with them continue to yield rewards for many years.

Planting an avenue of shade trees along a busy road is a helpful metaphor for leaving a long-lasting financial legacy. The individual planting the trees is aware that future travelers might reap the biggest rewards and that complete growth will require patience. For the benefit of tomorrow, each tree symbolizes a deliberate choice made now. Many others benefit from sun protection years later without ever having met the person who planted the trees. Financial stewardship functions similarly. Every wise choice made, every lesson imparted, every chance generated, and every deed of kindness creates another tree that offers consolation, direction, and strength to those who come after. With constant attention, a significant legacy develops subtly until its impact far outweighs the initial endeavor.

Use the Legacy Action Framework to start putting these concepts into practice right away. Start by deciding what values you wish to convey to future generations through your financial life. Think about traits like accountability, kindness, self-control, honesty, patience, thankfulness, and prudent stewardship. Next, arrange your crucial financial data so that, should the necessity arise, family members may comprehend your intentions. Examine long-term goals, insurance, savings, investments, and legal documents to make sure they are up to date and properly recorded. Continue by giving loved ones regular opportunities to talk about financial responsibility through real-world discussions and shared experiences rather than sporadic lectures. Consistently exhibit sound financial practices because it is sometimes more beneficial to teach by example than by words alone. Lastly, evaluate your plans annually and modify them if your priorities, financial objectives, and family situation change. Continue doing this throughout your life to ensure that your financial legacy reflects your principles and long-term goals.

This framework's strength is its focus on both preparation and modeling. Organizing financial resources receives a lot of attention, but teaching the concepts needed to manage them prudently is often neglected. Others impart insightful knowledge while ignoring useful planning. Both are necessary for long-lasting impact. Financial resources are safeguarded by clear planning, and people are trained to use them appropriately by setting a consistent example. When they work together, they leave behind a legacy that will be important for future generations and changing circumstances.

Realizing that everyone may leave a significant financial legacy, regardless of income or collected wealth, is another crucial lesson. Some people erroneously think that legacy planning is limited to people with significant financial resources. In actuality, everyone leaves behind behaviors, morals, choices, and models that affect other people. A legacy that goes well beyond money is created by teaching kids to save on a regular basis, modeling sound financial conduct, helping out the community, keeping your word, and making responsible plans. A family's character is frequently its most significant inheritance.

In order to have a lasting impact, patience is also crucial. It takes years for many financial habits to show their full benefits. Investments increase over time. Repeated acts build trust. Over time, family customs become stronger. Experience deepens wisdom. People who are dedicated to long-term thinking are aware that significant impact is rarely produced by dramatic events. Through consistent, everyday choices made year after year, it increases steadily. Even when the consequences are not immediately apparent, every conscientious action improves the future.

It is equally crucial to realize that a lasting legacy is always changing. Thoughtful modifications may be necessary due to new experiences, evolving family demands, and unforeseen possibilities. Financial plans can continue to be effective while upholding their guiding principles when they are flexible. Regularly reviewing goals guarantees that personal priorities and practical arrangements continue to reflect current circumstances without losing sight of the greater purpose behind every choice.

Consider what values your present financial practices convey to people who see you make daily choices. Which financial lesson would you most like the next generation to keep in mind and apply to their own lives? What doable action may you take this month better to arrange your financial goals for your family's benefit? If you purposefully shared your financial expertise and experience, how might your loved ones or community benefit? What long-term impact do you expect your financial choices will continue to have in many years?

Every financial journey is most fulfilling when one's own achievement results in long-term benefits for others. Opportunities that last much beyond your lifetime could be created by the habits you have formed, the knowledge you have acquired, and the resources you have wisely handled. Keep leading a purposeful, disciplined, and giving life, realizing that each deliberate choice you make enhances the future you are contributing to. One outstanding accomplishment never completes the journey toward enduring influence. It is the result of innumerable persistent acts motivated by integrity, purpose, and compassion. As your journey progresses, let every financial decision you make represent both the life you want to lead now and the lasting legacy you hope will uplift, safeguard, and inspire future generations.

CONCLUSION

Reaching the completion of this trip marks the start of a lifetime commitment to making better decisions every day rather than the conclusion of your financial success. The ideas discussed in these chapters show that patience, consistency, discipline, and deliberate action—rather than rapid outcomes—are the keys to building long-term prosperity. Your capacity to build more independence, stability, and self-assurance for yourself and the people you love most is strengthened by each good financial habit you adopt.

Only when you constantly use the knowledge you have acquired in your daily life does it become valuable. While thoughtful planning equips you for both possibilities and unforeseen obstacles, small adjustments made repeatedly over time result in significant progress. Regardless of shifting conditions, you may continue to improve your financial future by staying committed to your objectives and making deliberate choices. Success is determined by your ability to keep learning, changing, and progressing rather than by your level of perfection.

Whenever you have to make financial decisions, let these teachings act as permanent guidance. Continue forming routines that uphold your principles, safeguard your advancement, and promote long-term thinking. You can inspire people by setting an example of prudent and disciplined financial stewardship and building a future characterized by stability, opportunity, and long-term prosperity with perseverance, accountability, and self-assurance.

Thank you for buying and reading/listening to our book. If you found this book useful/helpful please take a few minutes and leave a review on the platform where you purchased our book. Your feedback matters greatly to us.

www.ingramcontent.com/pod-product-compliance
Lightning Source LLC
LaVergne TN
LVHW050810061126
851857LV00012B/754
* 9 7 9 8 2 5 6 2 8 9 5 6 0 *